"The ability to give and receive love is t[...] ing healthy relationships. Some of us fi[...] find it extremely difficult. In this book, Dr. Anita Knight Kuhnley explains why and points readers toward the pathway to self-understanding and learning how to enhance their ability to build intimate relationships."

Gary Chapman, PhD, author of *The 5 Love Languages*

"Healthy relationships are critical for happiness, well-being, and even brain health. *The Four Relationship Styles* gives readers the tools they need to build and maintain secure attachments that enhance their connections with others so they can experience more love in their lives."

Daniel Amen, MD, author of *Change Your Brain Every Day*

"*The Four Relationship Styles* should be required reading! We recommend it to all of our clients on their journey to become more self-aware."

Ellen Fein and Sherrie Schneider, dating coaches and bestselling coauthors of *The Rules*, *Not Your Mother's Rules*, and *The Rules Handbook*

"Dr. Anita Knight Kuhnley takes classic attachment theory and masterfully applies it by guiding her readers in how to understand themselves and those with whom they seek to be in relationships. Blending both research and years of clinical application, she demonstrates how the attachment styles can accurately predict both relationship satisfaction and longevity. Techniques for creating secure relationships adapted to each relational style are thoroughly explained, helping the reader achieve deeper and more satisfying relationships. Highly recommended!"

Kenyon Knapp, PhD, LPC, dean of the school of behavioral sciences at Liberty University

THE
FOUR
RELATIONSHIP
STYLES

How **Attachment Theory**
Can Help You in Your Search for Lasting Love

DR. ANITA KNIGHT KUHNLEY

BakerBooks
a division of Baker Publishing Group
Grand Rapids, Michigan

Published by Baker Books
a division of Baker Publishing Group
Grand Rapids, Michigan
BakerBooks.com

Printed in the United States of America

Library of Congress Cataloging-in-Publication Data
Names: Kuhnley, Anita Knight, 1980– author.
Title: The four relationship styles : how attachment theory can help you in your
    search for lasting love / Dr. Anita Knight Kuhnley.
Description: Grand Rapids, Michigan : Baker Books, a division of Baker Publishing
    Group, [2024] | Includes bibliographical references.
Identifiers: LCCN 2023014294 | ISBN 9781540902887 (paper) | ISBN 9781540903907
    (casebound) | ISBN 9781493444137 (ebook)
Subjects: LCSH: Intimacy (Psychology) | Interpersonal relations. | Dating (Social
    customs) | Attachment behavior.
Classification: LCC HQ801 .K8538 2024 | DDC 306.73—dc23/eng/20230531
LC record available at https://lccn.loc.gov/2023014294

Some names and details have been changed to protect the privacy of the individuals involved.

The author is represented by James D. Hart.

Baker Publishing Group publications use paper produced from sustainable forestry practices and post-consumer waste whenever possible.

24   25   26   27   28   29   30   7   6   5   4   3   2   1

To my teachers and mentors
who have led the way on this journey of becoming—
Dr. George Jefferson, Dr. Gary Sibcy,
Amy Beldin, and Stephen Parker.
I owe you a debt of gratitude.

CONTENTS

Foreword: Created for Relationship   9

Introduction: The Science of Attachment Theory   13

1. What Are Relationship Styles?   19
2. The Circle of Security   40
3. Identifying Your Relationship Style   50
4. The Firefighter   77
5. The Investigator   103
6. The Security Guard   132
7. The Networker   157
8. The Path to Connection   181

Glossary   205
Acknowledgments   210
Notes   216

FOREWORD

Created for Relationship

We were created *in* relationship, *through* relationship, and *for* relationship. The Genesis story opens with a palette of un-limited splendor, a breathtaking expression of the Creator and His nature. Much like an artist, God steps back for a better perspective—His passion and glory emerging on a canvas that was once empty and void. These are words of light and life spoken before the darkness. The design is "good" (1:25). The joy is definitive. This is followed by a crowning achievement, His image bearer formed out of the very dust of the earth, and behold, God declares him to be "very good" (1:31). He "breathed into his nostrils the breath of life, and the man became a living being" (2:7). Then the determination is made that something is "not good" (2:18)—the man is alone and has no outlet for the beauty and relational intimacy found in the Trinity. The great and resourceful Creator solves this problem by creating a suitable partner, a romantic attachment figure, if you will, for Adam. Her name is Eve.

When Adam and Eve sin against the Lord in the garden, unfettered relationship with the Creator is broken, as is a measure of trust and security between the man and the woman. When God asks, "Where are you?," Adam responds, "I heard you in the garden, and I was afraid because I was naked; so I hid" (3:10). Ever since the fall of humankind, when we're aware of our own "nakedness," not in the literal sense but when we fail, come up short, experience pain, feel alone, or are rejected by others, our natural tendency is to be afraid and ashamed, and we begin looking—both physically and metaphorically—for a place to hide.

The truth is that far too often, we have a crisis of identity and are insecure with the man or woman in the mirror. Before long, the insecurity spreads in how we relate (or don't relate) to others, including God, and we seek ways to compensate, protect ourselves, and bring greater balance into our lives; we desperately seek the safety of trusting and caring relationships that we hope will bring a measure of affirmation, validation, or love. This is the essence of *The Four Relationship Styles* by Dr. Anita Knight Kuhnley, a thorough, timely, and well-researched discourse on the critical importance of having and maintaining healthy relationships in life.

Some argue that even though this generation is the most technologically connected in history, it is also the most relationally disconnected generation in history. The trend across generations reveals an ever-widening gap—from the Silent Generation (1928–1945), to Baby Boomers (1946–1964), to Generation X (1965–1980), to Millennials (1981–1996), and now to Generation Z (1997–2012) and beyond. Besides this growing disparity, we've also contended with a three-year global pandemic. If COVID-19 was the earthquake that shook the world, then the subsequent mental health crisis is the tsunami that followed. Every related statistic—loneliness, anxiety, depression, suicide, abuse, domestic violence, addictive disorders, marital and family stress—has skyrocketed, and knowing no boundaries, the impact has also penetrated the walls of the church. As a result of extended social distancing and human isolation, people everywhere were prevented from the very thing their God-given DNA was designed for—connection and relationship.

When it comes to the field of helping people—from lay caregiving and chaplaincy to life coaching, social work, and licensed mental health practice—the ability to form a therapeutic bond is often seen as one of the most important tasks leading to breakthrough, recovery, greater well-being, and personal growth. Research has clearly revealed that one of the greatest determining factors related to positive treatment outcomes has to do with the quality of relationship between the one seeking help and the one offering help. In many regards, the same dynamic also comes into play when considering everyday relationships . . . within a marriage, among family members, between friends or coworkers, in business transactions, between leaders and their stakeholders, and more.

The Four Relationship Styles offers readers, in both their personal and professional roles, an opportunity to grow in self-awareness and have a better grasp of how they form and maintain significant attachments. This eight-chapter pathway to discovering greater and more meaningful connectedness with others is becoming an increasingly critical life skill in our fast-paced, push-button, instant-everything, post-COVID world.

When I lived in California years ago, I used to do quite a bit of rock climbing with at-risk teens who lacked any meaningful connections in their lives. There are a number of essential voice commands climbers utilize, especially when there is limited or no visual contact between them. Whether climbing or rappelling, "On belay" is the first command used, and it refers to different techniques for keeping sufficient tension on a climbing rope so that in the event of a mishap, a climber won't fall very far before being safely caught and supported. The command indicates the climber is now connected to the rope. The partner responds by saying, "Belay on," which conveys the equally important message, "I'm locked in and anchored here for you ... for your safety, your security, and your well-being. I have you and you're good to go!"

Mountains, like obstacles and even relationships, can be successfully summited with determination, teamwork, support, consistent communication, and most of all, the element of trust. The same is true for people facing loss, trauma, crisis, or simply a time when hope has vanished and guidance is needed. Segments of humanity continue to struggle with the right approach, the right resources, and the right navigation tools for safe and secure relationships. So, how do you say, "Belay on"? Start reading ... and clip in to the rope with the chapters that follow.

Eric Scalise, PhD, senior vice president and chief strategy officer, Hope for the Heart, and president, LIV Consulting, LLC

INTRODUCTION

The Science of Attachment Theory

How are you doing, neighbor? I mean, how is your heart? We've had some difficult times in our world lately. For many of us, that's activated our need for a safe place for comfort and perhaps a warm embrace.

One of the few constants in life is that things change. I've often resisted this idea. I never liked the last day of school growing up. It meant saying goodbye to my classmates for the summer and saying goodbye to the teacher who had helped me learn. As an adult, it's been even harder saying goodbye to loved ones, like my grandmother Jean, who died long before her time, and my other grandmother, Mims, who lived to be ninety-one years young.

It wasn't until I studied attachment theory that I realized the significance of this pattern. Just after my Mims died, I recall my cousin Adam saying, "It is hard to imagine a world without Mims." This statement signifies the beginning of an important process we must all go through to align our inner worlds with the changes that have happened in our outer worlds. Loss is an inherently disorganizing experience; it can require us to reorganize our inner center—what attachment researchers often call our "secure base" and "safe haven." We often need support in organizing our feelings and adjusting to the new world without our loved one in it. Or in accepting someone new into our circle.

If you've ever owned a car, you know it comes with an owner's manual, complete with a manufacturer's guide about when to change spark plugs and power steering fluid. Though relationships are some of the most important experiences in life, they don't come with a manual. And we tend to follow the same guidebook that we subconsciously crafted for ourselves in childhood. However, we do have the science of attachment theory, which defines attachment styles (also known as relationship styles) and explains how they predict the majority of our relationship experiences.

Humans are wired for the comfort of community and relationship, and yet those connections can be elusive if our early life experiences didn't provide us with responsive caregivers who taught us that people would be there to love and care for us.

Perhaps you've found that you and your partner love each other very much but you don't always love each other very well.

Maybe you've found romantic relationships challenging in your adult years. Perhaps you've found that you and your partner love each other very much but you don't always love each other very well. I've certainly found myself facing a lot of hills and valleys in relationships and have longed to understand why some work so well and others seem to fail.

A Quest to Understand Relationships

Nearly two decades ago, I was overseeing a college counseling center where I supervised and trained counselors. During my graduate training, I encountered someone who would be one of the most influential figures in my professional career. I had a mentor named Dr. George Jefferson who not only taught me the skills of a master therapist and how to coach students but also showed me God's love with skin on—praying for me, blessing me, and starting me on a lifelong coffee habit. Every morning, he would ask me if I wanted coffee, and I would say, "No, I'm fine." Then he would reply, "I didn't ask you how you were doing. I asked if you wanted coffee." It was not long before I became a coffee aficionado.

Even now, nearly twenty years after that first cup of coffee, the taste of black coffee reminds me of the loving-kindness of God, a safe haven, and an optimal learning environment. Dr. J and I had some great laughs, and he always checked in with me on how I was feeling. He prayed for me and encouraged me. Those were tremendous years of growth not only professionally but in personal awareness and attachment security as well.

A Different Story

My first marriage relationship was a different story. It was filled with hills and valleys. That relationship ended in divorce, which was heart-wrenching for me. I was concerned I had failed God, and I had lots of questions. I had heard people say that God hates divorce, and at that time I wondered, "Since God hates divorce, does he now hate me too?"

I had a powerful conversation with a colleague about this question after one of my conference presentations. He shared that he once saw a television interview where a television host asked Billy Graham what he'd do if his son was gay. Graham answered, "I would love him." As the host went on, Graham stopped him and went back and said, "No wait, I would love him *more!*" My colleague said that's what he imagined God was like. He said that if you've gone through a divorce, God would say not only does he still love you but he loves you more.

This wasn't the first divorce that hurt me. I'd been impacted by divorce as a child once, too, and that left me with feelings of lingering sadness. When I started studying in the school of psychology and counseling, I had a pivotal discussion with a professor named Dr. Eric Scalise. Dr. Scalise handed me a book that would start my twenty-year journey into conducting and unpacking research to reveal the dynamics and influence of attachment styles. The book was on the topic of attachment. It sparked my appreciation for relationship science. Since I picked up that book, I haven't stopped studying attachment theory.

That interaction with Dr. Scalise changed my life. It was the beginning of a lifelong research journey to discover the path toward secure relationships. Armed with my desire to avoid the painful endings of relationships gone wrong and to do whatever I could to help others avoid the pain I experienced and the pain that can come from navigating the sometimes-painful waters of human relationships, I set out on a quest to find the answers to why some relationships worked out well and others did not and how to help people experience more of the former. The tools in my tool kit included psychological principles, careful research, and experience conducting therapy. Eventually I was able to add certification in assessing adult attachment styles. Armed with these tools and the Lord's guidance, it became my goal to formulate a path home to security. The scientific studies I read were full of information about what went wrong in attachment relationships, and there was even content on what needed to change, but there was a gap in how. So, with a research team of students and colleagues, I began the process of unveiling how the science of attachment explains so much about our relationships and offers the language of relationship styles as a method for communicating about relationship needs. It also provides practical strategies that make it easy to apply the science of attachment so that people can use it to make their relationships bloom and flourish.

This book is the culmination of all my study and research among the best scholars in the area of attachment and relationship science, and it's the culmination of my quest to help others avoid the suffering that's often associated with relationships gone wrong (and that I came to know all too well). Attachment theory explains much of our relationship behavior and can help us sort out even the messiest relationship dynamics. It takes work to cultivate awareness because we must be willing to face the truth of our stories. It is important to remember that the journey can sometimes take a circuitous route, though with God, we are always moving forward.

This book will help you identify where you are and where you want to be, as well as share some practical strategies for getting to your destination. In the field of counseling, we call this "the journey of becoming"[1] because we often find that the journey, and what we learn along the way, is just as important as the destination and application.

> *It takes work to cultivate awareness because we must be willing to face the truth of our stories.*

The scholarship informing this book is based on years of research combined with classical attachment theory,[2] modern attachment theory,[3] God attachment, and the unchanging truth of God's Word. I hope you find that, like a cup of hot cocoa on a cold day or the comfort of the *Mister Rogers' Neighborhood* theme song, this book is a friendly companion on your journey toward getting to know yourself better and making the most of your romantic relationship style so that you can experience loving relationships along the way. So, take a moment to pour yourself your favorite cozy beverage, and let's dive in.

1

What Are Relationship Styles?

How good are you at the relationship game? Friends, parents, spouses, children ... It seems some people are pros, and the rest of us do our best to connect with others with varying degrees of success.

But what if you could predict—with over 70 percent accuracy—whether your future children (if you have any) will be inclined to move toward secure relationships, get tangled up in relationships, or avoid relationships altogether?[1] And what if you could anticipate whether you and your date are more likely to move toward deep connection or disconnection?[2] Or that you were likely to unintentionally sabotage a relationship you'd like to maintain? What if you'd just like to improve your romantic relationships?

If you could, would you be interested in an assessment/quiz that could help you answer these questions with research-backed support and a road map to guide you on a journey with the *science of connection*? If your answer is yes, I have good news for you. The science of attachment offers a great deal of understanding about our relationship patterns and the way we connect with others, such as:

- why we follow certain interaction patterns in relationships
- why we turn toward or away from connection
- how we are impacted by our relationship partners and histories to be compelled toward deep connection, to pull away, or to get tangled up
- why some relationships seem to be so full of drama while others are easy and seamless
- how the way we narrate our relationship histories colors our current relationships

Relationship science reveals that romantic relationships follow certain patterns that we are likely to miss without training and study. However, scholars in relationship science have found that if we participate in certain practices, we can predict, with over 91 percent accuracy, whether our relationships will flourish like the cedars of Lebanon or be doomed to destruction.

One of the great predictors associated with relationship bliss is our relationship style, specifically the direction and patterns that style motivates us to engage in. In the pages that follow, we will discuss how to optimize our relationship styles so that they work for us and lead us on a path toward the relationship we have always wanted. We will discuss how to identify our relationship style (chap. 3), the needs and unique features of our current relationship style (chaps. 4–7), and potential pitfalls with some partners based on relationship style considerations (chap. 8). The final chapter will also cover the promising patterns with other potential partners and how to optimize our relationship style by clearly communicating our needs and showing up as the best version of ourselves in relationships.

Why Predicting Relationship Outcomes Is Important

Rose was a typical five-year-old, who was full of the joy of life. She and her divorced mother, Cruella, lived with Rose's grandmother in an old home with a big backyard. But one day Cruella announced that she and Rose would be moving in with Cruella's tall, dark, and handsome boyfriend.

Cruella was in love, and she couldn't see that her boyfriend wasn't thrilled to have Rose around. He glared at her, he shouted at her, and eventually he slapped her. Rose became preoccupied with fear and worried she might say or do the wrong thing. She began having difficulties at school, she was no longer interested in play, and she was fidgety. When Cruella discovered the abuse, she ended the relationship, moved them back in with her mother, and began going to counseling.

I encountered Rose at age seven; she was one of my earliest clients. She first came to play therapy while her mother was getting counseling from a colleague of mine. I worked with Rose for many years. We identified safe and secure people who had offered her expressions of care, such as her grandfather. We helped her find her own voice, as well as safety, healing, and a more secure relationship style. (The road was a circuitous one, and her rocky relationship with Cruella sometimes proved a challenge. When Rose was a teenager, for example, Cruella disappeared and left her on her own.)

Rose's life demonstrates how challenging it can be to navigate life's ups and downs when you do not have a safe haven—a secure base—to retreat to during stressful times or to explore the world from.

Without intervention, Rose would likely have replicated the relationships of Cruella and would also have been too preoccupied with her own relationships to engage and explore the world around her or protect her loved ones when needed. Rose would likely have replicated unhealthy dynamics that could create an emotional cradle of anger and hostility for any of her own future children. Instead, though, she has revised her relationship blueprint to believe that she can give and receive love from others, and she has a vibrant relationship with her husband and business partner, Stephen. This would not have been possible without Rose's willingness to lean into the discomfort and do the hard work of optimizing her relationship style.

If you grew up as a child of divorce, you may be inclined to think, "I would do anything to avoid having a marriage that ended like that of my parents!" or "I do not want my children to experience what I went through as a child of divorce." Scholars of relationship science have found that children who grew up in a home with marital distress and conflict have a greater likelihood of experiencing health struggles, depression, difficulties with social competence, withdrawal, problems with academic performance, and challenges related to conduct.[3]

We tend to replicate our parents' style of relating. However, there is good news: *it does not have to be this way.* Using the abundance of relationship science research, we can now identify the patterns and relationship styles that couples who are likely to have great success used compared to those who find their relationships suffering. Those who succeed at relationships do some things very differently from those who have trouble with them—and this shows up in their relationship styles.

The good news is you are not stuck repeating the same steps that leave you dancing alone or among the worst of the amateur partners available. You can become a relationship pro and optimize your relationship style with some key adjustments to your relationship blueprint that will help you attract another relationship pro. It is not a quick fix or always a straight and smooth road, but it is an adventure that will ensure you will not always have to dance on your own.

How Is It Possible to Predict the Outcome of Relationships?

In order to predict relationship outcomes, we must first observe the relational circumstances. One helpful way to do this is to identify your current relationship style (see chap. 3). The next step is to understand the inner workings of that particular relationship style (see chaps. 4–7). It is also important to gain an understanding of your partner's style and the way your two styles are likely to interact. This information will answer the question, Does the couple turn toward or away from each other during times of distress? The answer to this question (and a few others that I will introduce in chap. 7) is part of the equation that predicts relationship success. In addition, developing a tool kit with a number of resources—such as your life verses, healing scripts (healing messages you can repeat in relationships, as if reading from a script), and helpful meditations—can all be strategic tools as you traverse this journey of becoming.

What Problems Come with Not Being Able to Predict the Outcomes of Relationships?

If we do not take the time to understand our relationship styles and the answers to our important questions as well as those of our partners, we do not give our relationships a fair shot. Without intentional editing of our relational scripts, we are wired to stay stuck. We are likely to continue using the same unhealthy relationship styles that were required for us to navigate childhood, despite them being overly ripe for our present circumstances.

If we do not take the time to reflect on our relational dynamics, we may not have the language to express our needs in a precise and intentional manner or the understanding to describe and make sense of our experiences. Gaining insight into our relationship styles may awaken in us an awareness to help us make sense of the sometimes chaotic world of relationships. This fresh engagement with newly created awareness can also offer an opportunity for us to discontinue the same cycles that were set in motion by those before us and that are keeping us stuck and feeling like we cannot find the love we need. It can also open new relational doors that were previously padlocked.

What Advantages Come with Being Able to Anticipate the Outcome of Relationships?

When we have an understanding of what our relationship style is, how our relationship style works, and what our partner's relationship style is, we can interact with greater empathy. Rather than taking it personally when our partner pushes us away, we may be able to hang on to a very important relationship tool from our tool kit—QTIP. We may be able to scrub away that waxy relational gunk that can keep us stuck and "quit taking it personally" when it comes to others' relational struggles. Perhaps we can visualize a grumpy partner as a young baby crying in their crib for hours while their caregiver goes out in the yard and simply ignores them. (Note: All babies cry for various reasons and are sometimes left alone to do so. But for some babies, this was their primary experience and the hallmark of their childhood. Their caregivers may have been taught not to pick up their baby every time they cried. Or they may have been inexperienced and overwhelmed.) As we look in our partner's eyes, perhaps instead of seeing a rude and cold human, we can see the little child who waited so long for a love that never came for them, thus teaching them to turn away from all relationships in order to self-protect. We may even be able to be a part of our partner's emotionally corrective healing experience and have them be a part of ours, and this knowledge and awareness may help us to move toward the relationship we desire.

Will We Be Anxious or at Peace in Our Romantic Relationships?

As it turns out, some research suggests our connections with our fathers shape how much anxiety we have in romantic relationships. But the good news is we can use various strategies to decrease relationship anxiety and increase relationship security.

Research conducted by Dr. Vered Shenaar-Golan, a professor in the department of social work at Tel-Hai Academic College in Galilee, Israel, and her colleagues examined a group of 148 fathers and their children (ages 8–18) at a hospital psychiatric center. The researchers gave the father-child pairs a variety of surveys to complete, including ones that specifically measured anxiety and avoidance relative to relationship styles. They found that there was a significant relationship between the father's anger and their children's anxiety and relationship styles characterized by anxiety.[4]

It's important to note that early relationships with fathers leave an imprint that can be hard to erase and rewrite. To predict whether a person can readily depend on romantic partners, we can look at a few key contributing experiences: how loving their childhood experiences with their fathers were, the degree to which they experienced pressure to achieve during childhood (surprisingly a positive predictor), and a lack of being angrily entangled with their mothers.

How Do We Start?

As mentioned earlier, the journey down the spiraled street of relationship interactions can straighten as we move toward optimizing our relationship style. The first step is to start with observing our own behavior and assessing ourselves (journaling and the assessment in chap. 3 can help), supporting our partner or future partner in doing the same, and reading the chapter that corresponds to our style and their style. This inquisition lends itself to an understanding of both the strengths and the challenges of our style, as well as the needs and answers to important questions so that we can work on other strategies to fill those needs. We will also be able to go into future relationships with eyes wide open, aware of how our relationship styles may help us connect, set us up to have extra conflict, or reinforce negative responses to one another's deepest questions. So, let's begin with understanding what relationship styles are.

Attachment Theory = Relationship Styles

Though we don't have a crystal ball for relationships, we do have the next best thing—some powerful predictive tools and a body of substantial research gathered over many decades.[5] And we now have powerful contemporary research that offers a guide and degree of certainty with some studies predicting, with over 91 percent certainty, whether a relationship will succeed or fail.[6] Among the behaviors associated with the slow, strong burn of a lasting romance is a relationship style that directs us down a straight line in a clear direction toward connection. We will peel back the layers of the relational onion to discuss the underlying dynamics, and as with peeling any onion, tissues may be in order. We will roll up our sleeves and take a deep dive into the typology of relationship styles as we advance our adventure together. However, to give you a sneak peek into the particulars, let's examine an example of how we can use relationship science to predict whether a relationship is relegated to a dead-end road, or redirected to a road toward romantic bliss. Those who have a relationship style that is characterized by a tendency to be lower in anxiety and higher in avoidance (which we call the Security Guard style) may tend to engage in a behavior called stonewalling, where in a conflict conversation a partner checks out and deactivates and disengages from the discussion. This is a behavior that predicts love will be lacking and the romantic flame is likely to fade away.

Knowing some key concepts that have consistently been linked toward detachment and, likewise behaviors linked toward optimal attachment, longevity, and satisfaction in relationships can help us identify and anticipate the dynamics of our relationships and know what is needed to advance or change our approach to relationships. Some of these necessary pieces of information include our relationship style, the relationship style of our partner, and the blueprint for our style that will help us forecast which relationships will be most healthy and fulfilling and will create the best atmosphere or "cradle" to hold our future children (and the inner children present in our relationships).

The relationship research that covers this critical content is called *attachment theory*, and it reveals how the relationship strategies and styles we develop in our childhood tend to persist into our adult relationships, often subconsciously.

There are four different attachment styles. Like an adaptogenic herb that helps our bodies adapt to a range of physical challenges, attachment styles help us adapt and roll with the wide range of relational punches that come our way.[7] Each style is a set of coping strategies that help us catch our breath when we take a relational punch in the gut. However, some relationship styles promote resilience faster than others, helping us get back on our feet and out of relational danger more expeditiously. Others may leave us down for the count.

It's important to take note of the heading above: attachment theory = relationship styles. To make sense of the extensive body of research and apply it in a practical and user-friendly way, we'll make a few language adjustments.

First, we will use the phrase *relationship styles* in place of *attachment styles*.

Second, each relationship style will be represented by a metaphor that represents the strategy most often used to meet that style's romantic relationship needs. Just as a job is a strategy to meet our financial needs in adulthood by helping us earn an income, a relationship style is a strategy to get our relational and emotional needs met.

The Four Relationship Styles

Let's take a quick look at the four relationship styles. Throughout this book we'll spend time unpacking each style to help bring a greater understanding of who you are as an individual and how you show up in relationships. Think of the four relationship styles like this: the Enneagram meets the five love languages with a rigorous scientific basis. The Enneagram is a compelling system that explains personality dynamics and underlying motivations. It is embraced by many but also criticized by some for a lack of research validity. And the five love languages, outlined in author Gary Chapman's book *The 5 Love Languages*, provide a framework for understanding how people like to give and receive love. The relationship styles we'll discuss in this book help to explain relationship dynamics and our tendencies when interacting with others; they also provide insight into deeply held beliefs about relationships and emotional needs and whether we move toward or away from romance.

Relationship researchers have used different terms when it comes to describing relationship styles, but they have commonly been referred to as the *fearful avoidant* style, the *preoccupied or entangled* style, the *dismissing or avoidant* style, and the *secure autonomous* style. For clarity, we will use job metaphors for each style to provide a mental picture of how they tend to manifest behaviorally during times of distress.

- The Firefighter (fearful avoidant style) has walked through relationship fires and often possesses an emotional depth. They have had to fight the fires of both the Security Guard and the Investigator.

- The Investigator (preoccupied or entangled style) is protective and on high alert, tends to silently scan the relational landscape with a watchful eye for perceived inconsistencies or unloving and rejecting behavior. They are anxious about relationships and often preoccupied with the details.

- The Security Guard (dismissing or avoidant style) tends to keep others at arm's length, is often focused on maintaining firm boundaries through distancing and independence, tends to use the term "normal" to describe relationship history, and can often be dismissing.

- The Networker (secure autonomous style) approaches relationships and seeks to connect readily.

In each of the relationship styles, there are those who are low-functioning and those who are high-functioning. It is important to conceptualize the styles on a continuum. For example, some Firefighters may have such high levels of anxiety that it radiates from them just as soon as they arrive in a room. Other Firefighters may experience some anxiety, but when you relate to them, it may seem more regulated, as if you are receiving their anxiety in a teacup. Their counterparts, on the other hand, seem to be encouraging you to drink their anxiety from a fire hose. Likewise, some relationship styles may be associated with greater levels of stability and satisfaction in romantic relationships. If a person is low-functioning in terms of their relationship style (especially if they are high in anxiety and/or avoidance), they are likely not aware of their responses to emotion, how they are triggered, or how their partners experience them. There are also those with high levels of security and low levels of anxiety and avoidance; there are people with a secure or insecure style. But it is not that simple. One of the goals of this text is to help increase security and become a high-functioning Firefighter, Investigator, Security Guard, or Networker.

We will take a deep dive into each of the four primary relationship styles in the coming chapters, but here is a sneak peek.

The Firefighter

The year is 1562, and the place is Verona, a large bustling city in northeastern Italy. Two families, Montague and Capulet, are entangled in a feud. Conversely, their offspring become entangled in a deeply felt romance. The tension crackles in the story of star-crossed lovers as we swing from scenes of humor to tragedy, paralleling the lovers' ecstasy of falling in love, the threat of separation, and the not-so-subtle sorrow of loss.

The male love interest, Romeo, finds himself caught up in acts of trespassing, murder, and other sins, while his female counterpart, Juliet, begs her parents to consider her feelings and needs but is rebuffed with no recourse. To deal with the backlash from their union, Juliet's family pressures her to marry someone else; instead, she takes a potion to put her in a death-like coma for "two and forty" hours to avoid the unwanted setup.

When Romeo discovers his beloved in her family's crypt, he assumes the worst and drinks poison in order to join Juliet in death. Upon awakening, Juliet is devastated to find Romeo is dead, and she uses his dagger to end her life. Their families finally settle their differences as a result of these tragic deaths.

Romeo and Juliet represent the struggle of the low-functioning Firefighter, who is prone to the impulsivity of fiery passion, the least-restrained goodbyes, emotion dysregulation, and family dysfunction and trauma—a path that without course correction leads to emotional death.

The Firefighter doesn't have a template for what to do in relationships when they're under stress or facing perceived danger. In order to connect or move toward others, they have to move toward relational danger and fire. Often in a double bind, Firefighters get caught debating the dilemma. Due to dangerous circumstances, they may have lost partners or experienced confusing situations where there was no one to go to for help. They may find themselves in situations they don't know how to navigate because their experiences have taught them that other people aren't trustworthy or dependable.

Firefighters have normal responses to abnormal situations.

To complicate things, they may also doubt their own worthiness and dependability. The Firefighter is both terrified and brave. In many ways, they share characteristics of the other three styles combined, yet they don't have one organized strategy for dealing with an activated attachment system. It isn't that there's something wrong with the Firefighter, though they're likely to conclude there is; rather, *there's something wrong with what happened to them.* Firefighters have normal responses to abnormal situations. The dangerous circumstances, the loss, or the abuse they experienced keep them in a hypervigilant and avoidant mode. They have the struggles and questions that both the Security Guard and the Investigator grapple with, but they may not have the same relational strategies these other styles have learned. The Firefighter faces the greatest challenge to finding the road to healthy connection.

The Investigator

In another tale of two lovers, Cleopatra and Antony are most often remembered as one of the most famous couples in history. Historians note that Cleopatra is the only woman alongside other household names from two thousand years ago, including Caesar, Plato, and Aristotle.[8] Shakespeare's rendition of Cleopatra and Antony's love story facilitated the couple's birth into the fictional world, where they joined the ranks of Romeo and Juliet in a dramatic and doomed romance.

In act 1, scene 1 of Shakespeare's play *Antony and Cleopatra*, Cleopatra's first utterance to Antony is flirtatious and teasing. She asks him a question that has been preoccupying her thoughts. She playfully presents it in jest, and the old proverb that "many a true word has been said in jest" is fitting in this case.[9] Cleopatra is looking for reassurance from Antony on a very important matter. She wants to know how much he loves her.

This is the question that preoccupies the heart of the Investigator, whose watchful eye is searching for the answer to that question in their relationships, scanning relational clues like an investigator scans a crime scene for evidence. The Investigator is an adept observer, sensitive to the subtleties of their partner's most nuanced responses. Like a bloodhound sniffing out a suspect, the Investigator sniffs out suspicions that their partner's love is lacking. Their investigative minds suspect and search for evidence to support their suspicions.

Like the Networker, who values relationships, the Investigator moves toward connection and prizes relationships. However, the Investigator has experienced inconsistent patterns in their history with important relationship figures. The Investigator's history has left them searching for any constant and, despite their observant eyes, they have come to one conclusion: the only consistency they can count on is that people are consistently inconsistent! Sometimes their caregivers or relationship partners were available and sensitive, and sometimes they were not available at all. This has left them searching for inconsistencies. The Investigator often analyzes interactions and gets tangled up in trying to make sense of inconsistent behaviors.

The only consistency they can count on is that people are consistently inconsistent!

Investigators often feel tidal waves of confusion sweeping them away from connecting with those they love romantically when they encounter the same perplexing phenomenon they experienced as a child. The best they can do to make sense of their experiences is to conclude that their relationship partners, like their childhood caregivers, are consistently inconsistent. Sometimes the Investigator gets tangled up in noticing inconsistent patterns of behavior, and they get preoccupied with anger or fear. If you ask them about childhood, they may slip into talking about the present, revealing some preoccupation. For example, they may say things like, "My mom used to compare me to my sister when I was a kid, but you know she still does that! Just the other day . . ."

All of these inconsistencies leave them with the nagging suspicion that something good is being withheld from them. Something that's required for children to naturally develop a secure relationship style is a reliable presence. But the Investigator's experiences have taught them mistrust. They've learned to doubt themselves, and the question that remains with them is whether they're worthy of love. It is always present in the back of their mind, with a twinge of pain at each inconsistent behavior they notice. This question leaves them with a tender and hollow spot in their heart—unfulfilled and longing. Despite assurances from their adult relationship partner, the hollow ache remains.

The Security Guard

The time was the nineteenth century, and playwright Edmond Rostand's dramatic story of unrequited love presented to the world—with great dramatic license—a seventeenth-century historical figure: Cyrano de Bergerac. Cyrano was known as a nobleman with two defining characteristics—one which he diligently worked to cultivate and refine, and the other, on his face.

Cyrano was a talented wordsmith and playwright whose vocabulary was known to be as large and cogent as his nose was long. Through a series of events, Cyrano became the mouthpiece for a less cogent speaker, Christian, in a romance with Christian's true love, Roxane. Unbeknownst to her, it was Cyrano's pen and prose that captivated Roxane's heart. Yet Cyrano managed to avoid sharing his true identity. Cyrano remained safe from exposure, and yet the walls that kept him safe from rejection were the same walls that kept him from finding his true love.

Like Cyrano, the Security Guard often erects walls to keep others out, and they guard those walls to ensure no one encroaches on their boundaries. On the outside, they seem cool, calm, and collected. However, like a duck that looks calm and serene as it swims along a stream while hidden just below the surface its legs flail about, so it is with the Security Guard: their interiority remains unseen by a seeing world.

On the outside, the Security Guard seems to be unfazed by abandonment and distancing by loved ones. Their relationship history is marred with a pervasive experience of rejection that tended to leave them alone and pushed away as a child and with unmet needs, and so they developed this style as a defensive mechanism. Their interiority is anything but smooth sailing, however, as they squirm to maintain their pretended poise. The Security Guard's walls keep them safe from the short-term pain of rejection but also block them from the long-term gain of connection. As a child who was turned away repeatedly, this rejection manifested in them, eventually causing them to turn away from romantic connection as adults and to keep people at arm's length. When

The Security Guard's walls keep them safe from the short-term pain of rejection but also block them from the long-term gain of connection.

it comes to relationship stress and conflict, they tend to avoid the very conversations needed to foster loving connection.

The Networker

In the summer of 1958 in the state of Virginia, sparks flew as a young couple fell in love. Mildred Jeter was a woman of Native American and African American descent, and Richard Loving was a white male.[10] Their relationship had developed from family friends to two people who longed to marry, but the law wasn't on their side.

During this time in history, anti-miscegenation laws forbade interracial marriages in the Commonwealth of Virginia. The young lovers embarked on a journey of eighty miles to legally marry in Washington, DC, and then returned home. The odds were stacked against them, and a mere five weeks after their matrimony, a sheriff invaded their home and threatened them with one year in prison or twenty-five years of exile from their home state.

They chose exile and fled back to Washington. Three children and five years later, they missed being near family and contacted an attorney. Volunteer attorneys offered to represent them and took their case all the way to the Supreme Court where there was a unanimous ruling that bans on interracial marriage were unconstitutional. *Loving vs. Virginia* was a landmark case.

The Lovings highly valued their relationship with one another and their family and friends. They were willing to explore options and overcome obstacles for the love they valued. As a result, they moved toward connection. Anxiety and avoidance didn't snuff out the spark of love that burned between them, and their love changed history. They nursed that spark into a torch they carried to light the path for those who would follow.

As we see with Richard and Mildred's case, a Networker doesn't feel much anxiety or avoidance with respect to relationships or painful emotions. Networkers have a favorable answer to the world's hidden ache because someone has taught them what love is and that they're worthy of that love. When they are stressed, they're quick to share their feelings with their relationship partners and receive comfort. They cling to those important relationships. Since they're quickly comforted, their attachment system turns off with ease, only requiring subtle reassurance from their important relationship partners to deactivate. Their heart is wild and free and ready to explore every corner of their environment. They take risks without much anxiety.

Networkers have a favorable answer to the world's hidden ache because someone has taught them what love is.

The Networker's internal compass brings them home to connection. They tend to trust easily and move toward relationships and connecting. Their relationship theme is an ode to a line from Alfred Lord Tennyson's poem "In Memoriam A. H. H.": "'Tis better to have loved and lost than never to have loved at all." Their narrative is one of valuing relationships and cherishing them as a pearl of great price. Their narrative is also replete with a balanced perspective and woven with coherence.

Organized and Disorganized Styles

The breakdown of the relationship styles into organized and disorganized styles means that those who have an organized style, the Networker, the Investigator, and the Security Guard— even if they're insecure as is the case for the Investigator and Security Guard—have clear strategies for how to handle painful emotions in the context of relationships. The Networker is considered secure, meaning they have an optimized relationship style.

The Firefighter faces the greatest challenge with both a disorganized and insecure relationship style and is characterized by unresolved loss or trauma, perhaps as a function of fearful interactions with early caregivers. The Firefighter is left with a challenging situation: to get help from their relationship partner, they have to go toward the fire and potentially get burned. Though the Firefighter may relate to aspects of each of the relationship styles, they generally have one primary style. Once a Firefighter resolves the loss or trauma they face, they will default to one of the three organized styles as their secondary strategy.

The Investigator gets tangled up in and preoccupied by overthinking why their relationship partners are inconsistent. They tend to get overwhelmed by emotion and preoccupied with feelings of anger or fear.

The Security Guard tends to push away emotions and seeks time away to deal with challenges.

The Networker moves toward feelings and toward other people for help and comfort to organize or process feelings in times of distress. Relationship researchers call the Networker's relationship style "secure, autonomous" meaning they have an optimized relationship style. Since their relationship history has demonstrated time and time again people will be there to give them the love and support they need, they have internalized this belief and can easily call on internal representations of present and past relationship figures to comfort themselves in times of distress. They are open to receive their partner's comfort and are quickly comforted. They have the courage to be vulnerable and share vulnerable feelings and are comforted quickly so they can return to their interests and explore.

The Creation of a Relationship Blueprint

John Bowlby, the British psychologist who pioneered attachment theory, determined that people have internal, mental working models. These internal models represent the external world through visual and verbal symbols[11]—which include the rules about how people act in relationships. These are conceptual explanations of how we *think* about relationships and where we stand in them. They have also been referred to as *relational schema*, *relationship rules*, and *cognitive models*. Here, we will call them *relationship blueprints*. Every human is born with a longing for the answers to two important questions, which make up our relationship blueprints: (1) Am I worthy of love? and (2) Can others be counted on to love me?

The way we ultimately behave in relationships—whether we move toward romance, away from it, or get tangled up in it—is a function of how we answer these questions. These answers also inform which relationship style we align with most. If our answers are no and no, we are a Firefighter. If our answers are no and yes, we are an Investigator. If our answers are yes and no, we are a Security Guard. If our answers to these questions are yes and yes, we are a Networker.

These deeply held subconscious beliefs can help us or hurt us. Sometimes we get in our own way and can be our own worst enemies. We can use relationship strategies, such as overanalyzing or avoiding, that are past their expiration dates even though our environments call for relational trust.

And yet, this isn't where the story ends: we can also be our biggest cheerleaders and help ourselves move toward change. God provides us with new opportunities and pathways toward connection if we're willing to take them. Perhaps as you read this book, you'll find yourself at one of those crossroads.

It takes a great deal of courage and vulnerability to face these relationship beliefs with honesty and do the hard work of revising your relationship blueprints where necessary. We don't have to remain stuck in the relationship styles we have. We can make them more secure. We don't have to keep reading from the same scripts, seeing the same dynamics arise with different partners.

KEY TAKEAWAYS

- The science of attachment offers a method for understanding relationship dynamics and has even been able to predict the future of relationship styles from one generation to the next.
- There are four different relationship styles: the Firefighter, the Investigator, the Security Guard, and the Networker.
- You are not stuck with the relationship style you have; you can make it better.
- Faith can be a resource on the journey of becoming your best self in relationships. God provides second chances and hope for healthy and fulfilling relationships.

A CONCEPT TO CONTEMPLATE

It's a lot to take in, isn't it? Consider making space to pause along this journey. You may have moments when you feel vulnerable and unsure of yourself; that's a good time to take out a journal and process your thoughts and feelings in words. Consider the following as you do:

> *And I am certain that God, who began the good work within you, will continue his work until it is finally finished on the day when Christ Jesus returns.*
>
> *Philippians 1:6 NLT*

2

The Circle of Security

Before we discuss the four relationship styles in depth, it's important to understand when and how they develop. The *when* is easy: childhood. That doesn't mean that anything about the relationship system is childish. On the contrary, it endures from the cradle to the grave and influences our romantic relationships in adulthood.

The *how* has to do with the signals we receive from our parents, caregivers, and other important relationship figures—our Circle of Security. Later in life, our romantic relationship styles are also impacted by stressors or loving messages that develop in our adult relationships, influencing our relationship style.

Before we take a deep dive into what relationship styles are and how they work, I want to highlight one important caveat: relationship styles are not personalities. Please keep this in mind.

You may have a warm and friendly temperament and love to connect with other people, but when you're under stress, your relationship style is activated, and you tend to retreat and push others away. For example, when little Johnny skinned his knee, did he go to Mom for comfort? Turn away to deal with it on his own? Or get tangled up in his response? His response is an indicator of his relationship style. You can think of these styles (the Firefighter, the Investigator, the Security Guard, and the Networker) as ways of meeting emotional and relational needs during times of stress.

This is demonstrated frequently in the church nursery. When a mom brings her child to the nursery and goes to leave, the child may protest her departure by crying, crawling after her, or seeking closeness somehow. These are called "attachment behaviors" because they're strategies a child uses to maintain proximity to their caregiver. Every human engages in attachment behaviors; we're hardwired to do so from childhood.

However, these behaviors look different in each of the four relationship styles. They are turned on or activated when a child *senses a threat*. Once they're reunited with their caregiver and receive comfort and a sense of felt safety, then they're ready to go out and explore their environment. When the attachment system switches off and the exploration system turns on, they can be present and attend to other things and engage in exploration.

This attachment figure (the term researchers often use to refer to the caregiver in childhood or a romantic partner in adulthood)—whether it's a parent or a caregiver—is the child's "secure base," and that relationship serves as their launching pad to explore the world. This is the ideal situation and is what my colleague Dr. Gary Sibcy calls Shouldville, where all is as it should be.[1] In Shouldville, when a child needs comfort, they encounter a comforting caregiver.

In Realville, however, this isn't always the case. If the child is feeling unsafe and seeks comfort but the caregiver isn't available, isn't responsive, or is abusive, the child's attachment system stays elevated, and their exploration system turns off. The attachment system remains on until the child achieves their goal of felt safety.[2]

Adults aren't much different. My husband, a board-certified child psychiatrist, likes to say that he works with "children age 3 to 103." He understands that we all have an inner child that needs to be tended to. Just like children, when an adult feels threatened, their attachment system is activated, and they begin to seek their romantic partner—or another attachment figure—to help them cope with the threat and retain the goal of felt safety.

So, what does an attachment figure look like for adults? Researchers have identified a few criteria a person has to meet to be an attachment figure. Some evidence suggests that adult romantic relationship partners need to possess these same characteristics: (1) serve as a person who is sought after for closeness, (2) serve as a safe haven while their partner is distressed and provide comfort and the alleviation of distress, and (3) serve as a secure base or launching pad from which their partner can feel confident to explore the outside world and environment and develop an autonomous personality.[3]

Other attachment researchers disagree about the concept of the safe haven and secure base in adulthood. Some believe that adults don't always have to serve that same safe haven capacity, since adults also ideally possess the capacity to regulate their own emotions and self-soothe during times of distress. Despite this lack of consensus, researchers agree that attachment styles and attachment needs are active from the cradle to the grave, and a number of different people can serve in the role of attachment figure throughout a person's life span. For example, attachment figures may include parents, grandparents, teachers, coaches, siblings, friends, significant others, spouses, and even God.

The Circle of Security

What happens when our relationship system isn't activated? The exploration system is activated, and we can be filled with awe and wonder as we explore our environment. Let's take a look at this in a visual format.

Figure 1.1

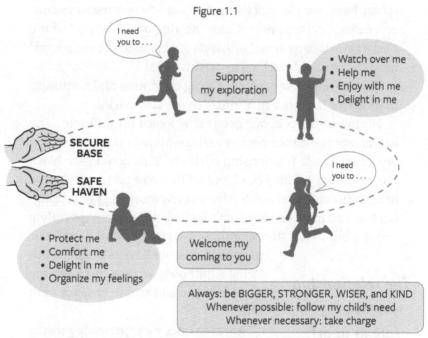

The Circle of Security modified from Bob Marvin and Wanda Seagroves' presentation at Liberty University. Used with permission from Kendall Hunt Publishing.

Figure 1.1 is called the Circle of Security, and it has been developed into a tool that Dr. Bob Marvin, a pioneering relationship researcher in the science of attachment, has used as a twenty-week-long therapeutic group to help caregivers. I have used it to train counselors how to assess where their client is in terms of level of system activation. The figure comes from *Research-Based Counseling Skills*, a book that counselors often read to develop the skills required to become a therapeutic person. The relationship system plays a role in nearly everything we do. Notice on the left side of the Circle of Security is a pair of hands. The hands represent our safe haven (open arms to retreat to during times of distress) and secure base (a launching pad from which we can explore the world). Our early relationship figures are often our first examples of a safe haven and secure base—or the lack thereof. Researchers sometimes conceptualize God attachment as a "nesting of the hands" where God's "everlasting arms" or hands are beneath the caregivers' hands, spiritually catching us (Deut. 33:27).[4]

This system is very active during childhood and continues to be active from our first inhale to our last exhale.

During adulthood, our needs may look a bit different. The hands represent the comfort and connection that are offered by our romantic relationship partners. This could look like a future spouse holding our hand while we're getting a shot or bringing us coffee when we have an early morning. Or us bringing them soup when they aren't feeling well or perhaps calling about a bill that's stressing them out. During childhood, our caregivers were our havens of safety, but during adulthood, we take turns serving as a safe haven and secure base for each other.

The relationship system plays a role in nearly everything we do.

However, once we experience a threat or stressor in our environment—a slight from a colleague, rejection from a friend, disappointing news, a traffic accident, or the loss of a loved one—our relationship system turns on and is activated, and we're then on the bottom side of the circle. Under stress, safety is our top priority. We're programmed to move toward our relationship partners and seek safety, comfort, and help organizing and processing our feelings. We need our relationship partners to welcome us. We need them to be comfortable with our vulnerability, help us sort through our emotions, and take delight in us. This life-giving cycle can allow us to reconnect, receive comfort, and feel loved, respected, and supported, and our relationship system can turn off again. When that happens, we are at the top of the circle and can turn our attention to our work and other activities.

When Our Safe Haven Is Not Available

Along the journey of becoming, many people experience hiccups when trying to access their safe haven and secure base. This leads to an unbecoming of sorts. When the relationship system is activated in children (and adults as well), they go into proximity-seeking mode and need help regulating painful emotions. If no one is there to help, they learn a painful truth. In these cases, they glean that their safe haven was not always safe, and this inconsistent availability leads to a state of heightened anxiety and preoccupation. They may experience rejection, harm, or danger. What happens when something goes wrong with the safe haven and secure base?

These factors lead to a specific relationship style. Let's look at the three relationship style patterns that emerge in these cases.

The Firefighter may have had one of two different types of safe havens or secure bases: (1) a very dangerous safe haven or secure base or (2) an unavailable or lost safe haven or secure base. Of the four relationship styles, the Firefighter had to be most resourceful when it came to dealing with an activated relationship system.

The Investigator's safe haven and secure base was consistently inconsistent. Sometimes these caregivers were available to provide a comforting response. Other times they were unavailable, neglectful, or rejecting. The Investigator learned to analyze the environment to determine which kind of caregiver they would get at any given moment.

The Security Guard experienced rejection from their caregivers and learned to minimize any sense of need and the activation of the relationship system. Their caregivers promoted premature independence, forcing them to the top of the circle before they were ready. Despite feigned independence, babies who tended to mask their needing behaviors using this style experienced just as much distress as those who did not. They just learned to hide it and turn away from their safe haven and secure base.

Note that the Networker emerges from a relatively consistent experience with caregivers that engenders trust and safety. They had the easiest time navigating their relationship system. The Networker's safe haven and secure base were consistently available, so they learned that others would be available to help and support them. They learned to be calmed and soothed quickly and easily. This helped them fine-tune their emotion-regulation skills, so they can quickly turn off the relationship system and turn on the exploration system. In some cases, a person may become an earned secure Networker (see chap. 8), despite some inconsistent or neglecting/unloving experiences in childhood. I call this the "But God" style. All the odds were stacked against them, and yet God brought someone into their life to show the child what love was, typically a grandparent, teacher, neighbor, coach, mentor, or even a babysitter.

A "Picture" of Attachment

Dr. Bob Marvin spoke at the university where I work, and my colleague and associate dean, Dr. Kevin Van Wynsberg, asked him the following question: "If you could share only one thing about attachment with counselors, what would it be?" Dr. Marvin said he would want counselors to see the following comic that depicts attachment in a nutshell.

Figure 1.2

In figure 1.2, we see a child feeling totally exhausted and depleted. Then the child encounters his safe haven, his open-armed caregiver, and the child goes to snuggle with Dad. This is the process of recharging the relationship system. Then we see the "full charge indicator wiggle," which, like the green full-battery bar on smartphones, represents the fully charged relationship system. The fully charged cells are ready for anything, and the boy bursts with exploration energy. Perhaps we could rename each of the five frames as follows: (1) attachment system activated, relational batteries depleted; (2) moving toward the safe haven; (3) recharging with some snuggle time; (4) attachment system turned off as relational batteries turn green and charge reaches 100 percent; (5) exploration system turned on; the child is ready to engage with the environment.

It's important to remember that the four relationship styles exist as a part of this system and not on their own. They're activated during times of stress and threat and can be turned off by "recharging" and having safety needs met. Again, this is much different from personality. A person may be social and enjoy engagement, but when their attachment system comes on, they tend to turn away from connection.

A Message of Hope

There is good news! You are not stuck with the relationship style you have—you can make it better! This is a message of hope. Your interpersonal history doesn't have to determine your interpersonal future. No one is destined to retain an orphaned spirit—unsafe and unloved in an unsafe and unloving world.

You are not stuck with the relationship style you have—you can make it better!

Previously we've been kept warm by the old, tattered blanket of doubt, self-blame, and independence. Perhaps that was all we had to cover ourselves during childhood. That old cover is now thin and unraveling. It will soon be seen for what it is. This thin fabric of doubt and suspicion, though comfortable and familiar, is too thin to keep us warm, cozy, and comforted. Instead, it leaves us lying exposed to the chilly pain of rejection, inconsistency, and self-doubt. Yet because we have been trying to wrap ourselves in this old thing for so long, we may not notice. We have perhaps become comfortable feeling uncomfortable.

Your relationships don't have to remain this way. God has planted within you the appropriate means to navigate relationships. And this book offers a new way to recognize what was always yours so that you can take cover with the warmth and safety provided by a healthy attachment system.

What does this journey look like in practical terms? Do little things pop up in your relationships that you wish you could solve? Or do you feel stuck in patterns of relating that are hard to change? Maybe you wonder why your partner always seems to shut down when you ask about spending more time together.

Take heart, there's hope—and relationship science offers little-known strategies that can have a large impact. In chapter 3, we'll look at how to find out where you are and identify the pathway home to connection.

KEY TAKEAWAYS

- Your relationship style emerges when your relationship system is activated. The Circle of Security is used to demonstrate the relationship system. When your relationship system is activated, you are on the bottom of the circle, but when your relational batteries are charged, it turns off and you move to the top of the circle.
- All relationship styles are activated during times of stress.
- The Networker has had trust-engendering experiences that nurture their capacity to easily regulate emotions.
- Relationship science offers hope that we can optimize our relationship style and move toward stronger and more secure connection.

A CONCEPT TO CONTEMPLATE

Your relationship style is activated when you are under pressure. Relationship styles predispose each of us to certain relationship *challenges* and certain relationship *strengths*. What triggers lead you to the bottom of the circle—to seeking security? Give it some thought and write about it in your journal. How can your faith be a resource when your relationship system is activated?

> *God is our refuge and strength, always ready to help in times of trouble.*
>
> Psalms 46:1 NLT

3

Identifying Your Relationship Style

In one of my first classes with the professor who would become a profound mentor to me, a student asked him, "Can I call you by your first name?"

Dr. George Jefferson replied, "Sure, you can call me by my first name. You can call me *Dr. J.*"

Another student asked if they really had to transcribe all the words in a counseling session verbatim on the "Verbatim Assignment." Dr. J replied, "No, you can do whatever you want to do, but if you would like to pass this class, then you need to follow these directions."

When I think about the sometimes uphill and often circuitous journey to developing greater levels of security in our relationship styles, I often think of Dr. J's words. We do not have to do hard things—we can do whatever we want in life. But if we want to "pass the class" or find success and satisfaction in relationships, then there is good news! Research reveals the insights and strategies we can use if we want to become more secure in our relationship styles. So that raises the questions: What does it take to become more secure in our relationship styles, and what are the rules and nature of "the game"?

Success and security in life and in relationships follow surprisingly different rules. Oftentimes women who are successful in work will struggle in relationships. Consider my colleague, who we will call Dr. X: She has earned three doctoral degrees, a therapist's license, and several multimillion-dollar grants, has a successful nonprofit organization that helps many people, and has run several marathons, just to get started. However, in the relationship department, her marriage deteriorated, her husband sued her for alimony, and she became overwhelmed by a dating world transformed by technology.

> *Success and security in life and in relationships follow surprisingly different rules.*

To many of her colleagues, she is the epitome of success; she knows how to set a goal and begin doing whatever it takes to accomplish it. When it comes to relationships though, this does not work quite as well. Thankfully, given her willingness to learn, her appreciation for education, and her faith, she is on a journey of becoming that involves reprioritizing, rebuilding, and revising some deeply held relationship scripts from the past, and she is currently in a satisfying dating relationship while she continues to work on her healing journey.

Authors Sherrie Schneider and Ellen Fein have written about a set of rules for dating and marriage and have emphasized the idea of gender roles in relationships, including that men are wired to pursue.[1] Interestingly, marriage therapist and researchers Drs. John and Julie Gottman's work has confirmed there is a pursue/withdraw pattern in each relationship, and often there are periods in every relationship where one partner pursues and one partner withdraws. Gottman and colleagues say,

"The avoider [what I've called the Security Guard] quickly feels that he or she has married an out-of-control crazy person. The volatile person [the Firefighter or Investigator] believes that he or she has married a cold fish and feels unloved, rejected, and unappreciated."[2] Gottman has discussed the idea that women often tend to pursue in the format of bringing up discussions about relationship concerns; the manner in which this is done is important, and a harsh start-up or pursuit can predict that a discussion will not go well and is not associated with longevity in relationships.

Schneider and Fein promote sensitivity to these gender roles and responsive behaviors for their female readers. They also share the caveat that women who are used to pursuing their goals in work and who pursue men with the same zeal may struggle in the relationship game. However, this set of sometimes controversial rules is not the only thing that sets the relationship game apart from other life pursuits. It is a different type of game altogether than most other pursuits.

Are Relationships a Finite or Infinite Game?

As motivational thought leader Simon Sinek explains in his book *The Infinite Game*, finite games are temporary. They have a beginning and an end, fixed rules, known players, and agreed-upon objectives. The objective of a finite game is clear: to win the game.

Infinite games are different. They require a different set of rules. They're bigger than us and our rules.[3] Trying to play an infinite game with a finite state of mind is a recipe for disaster.

Sinek lays out the criteria for an infinite game pretty clearly. First there must be two or more players. Relationship styles, like relationships, are influenced by the nature of an infinite game. Second, unlike the finite game of boxing, where there are winners and losers, a person with a secure relationship style, like the Networker, has a clear advantage in the infinite game as they consciously or subconsciously understand the nature of the game more than their comrades who have not optimized their relationship styles.

There are many choice points along the road of life where we make decisions that strongly influence our life's trajectory and our ultimate destination. Imagine yourself as the character in Robert Frost's poem about two roads diverging in a "yellow wood." The air is cool and crisp, and you can feel the breeze blowing through your hair. After admiring the beauty of the "yellow wood," you fix your eyes on the fork in the road and reflect on Frost's lament about having to choose just one path. You ponder which path (or perhaps which date or decision about dating) is the best for you.

You take time to deliberate. As you think about the relational dilemma you're currently facing, you wonder how to respond. But what if you didn't have to wonder? What if you could instinctively know—based on what you know about yourself and your relationship style—and reflect back years later, thankful that you took the path that was best?

As we discussed in chapter 1, there are four different relationship styles, and you can learn to *optimize* your style—meaning you can be high-functioning within a given set of behavioral patterns *and* you can continue to grow and cultivate your awareness so that you live with intention, bringing your responses into greater and greater alignment with your desired relationship outcomes.

The person with an optimized relationship style has instincts about which path to choose when they arrive at a relational fork in the road. When two roads diverge, they readily recognize the path of the infinite game in one direction and the path of the finite game heading in the other. They won't stop and stare down both paths, lamenting being one traveler with two equally appealing options, because they have an instinctual homing device helping them select the optimal path for the infinite game. They have cultivated awareness about their natural tendencies, identified environmental and relational triggers, and are aware of the tendencies of their loved ones. They are willing to lean into the discomfort of sharing, learning from, and understanding uncomfortable feelings and relational situations. They are in tune with their relational system.

Two Camps of Thought

The science of attachment is one of the most extensively studied scientific theories on human relationships. Those who study this approach typically fall into one of two camps. One group of researchers looked at parent-child bonds and how they interact and identify attachment styles. This was evidenced by the way small children interacted in a nursery when their mother left the room and again when she returned. These experiments, conducted in the 1970s, were given an interesting name: The Strange Situation.

These researchers have also studied adult attachment and how relationship styles manifest throughout an interview by analyzing the adult speaker's state of mind. They found that when asked to describe their early relationships with their parents or caregivers, the way adults talked about their relationship history predicted how they'd interact with their children years later.[4]

Researchers in the second camp of thought looked at romantic attachment.[5] Many of the same rules apply. In romantic attachment, relationship partners take turns serving as safe haven and secure base for one another, so the caregiving system is also involved.

Testing to Determine Your Relationship Style

There are several different models for thinking about and measuring relationship styles. Let's take a moment to briefly touch on how the scientific literature addresses attachment measurement before we dive into the specifics and the test itself. Research on relationship styles has included two different streams of thought, which come together in this text: parent-child relationship styles and romantic relationship styles. Both are influenced by our relationship histories and our childhood relationships. Some research has postulated that our romantic attachment has origins with the parent of the opposite sex.[6]

Tests for measuring relationship styles also deal with techniques for emotion regulation. Modern attachment therapists have even begun identifying relationship styles and emotion management traits as one and the same. Managing emotions has been referred to using "hyper-activating" (heightening emotions) and "deactivating" (calming or reducing the intensity of emotions) strategies.[7]

As far as how relationship styles are measured, there is some disagreement among researchers that indicates the official Adult Attachment Interview (AAI has been considered by some a gold standard, as it includes a one-hour interview that is then transcribed and thoroughly coded by a trained coder who is highly reliable; we will discuss this later in the text) and any self-survey measures of romantic attachment aren't connected or correlated, but Dr. Phillip Shaver of the department of psychology at the University of California–Davis and his colleagues believe this is likely due to small samples and challenges in research design since much other research suggests they *are* related.[8] To develop an accurate but brief test for this book, I have worked with a research team of experts in relationship science and valid survey methods (known in the scientific literature as attachment theory and psychometrics). For a longer, more comprehensive and nuanced assessment that is in development, please see my website, DrAnitaKuhnley .com.

Job Metaphors for Relationship Styles

The figure below illustrates the four relationship styles. As you can see, the y-axis (vertical) represents the blueprint (or belief) for whether the self is worthy of love. You'll notice that the pointed arrows or corners represent a continuum. At the top of the y-axis is the belief that the self is worthy of love, and at the bottom is the belief that the self is unworthy of love.

The x-axis (horizontal) represents our other relationship blueprint: what we've come to expect and "know emotionally" regarding others in terms of their ability to show us love and care. The positive, or right side, of the x-axis represents the belief that others can show love, and the negative, or left side, of the x-axis represents the belief that others can't show love.

The Networker (pictured at the top right of figure 3.1) looks at others with open arms, easily trusting and embracing connection. They believe they're worthy of love and that others are able to show them the love they need. Often, their relationship histories have taught them this is true. Their relationship narrative tends to be balanced and free of blame, and their sense of humor is often intact.

Those with the Investigator's style (bottom right) believe that others are more than able to show love, but this belief is counteracted by the belief that they choose not to show love *to them* because the Investigator believes they are unworthy of love. The Investigator may have experienced inconsistent parenting, role reversals where they were responsible for emotionally caring for their caregivers, and other situations that preoccupied them with anger or fear.

The Security Guard's style (top left) is characterized by a belief that others aren't competent to show love but that the self is worthy of love. Their histories are wrought with rejection and caregivers who pushed them away. Security Guards keep others at arm's length and turn away from connection.

The Firefighter's (bottom left) beliefs about their own worthiness of love and others' capacity to love them are negative on both sides of the equation. As my dear colleagues Dr. Gary Sibcy and Tim Clinton like to say, "The grass is dead on both sides of the fence." Their relationship history may have involved scary experiences with early caregivers, or they may have experienced loss or abusive experiences at the hands of their caregivers.

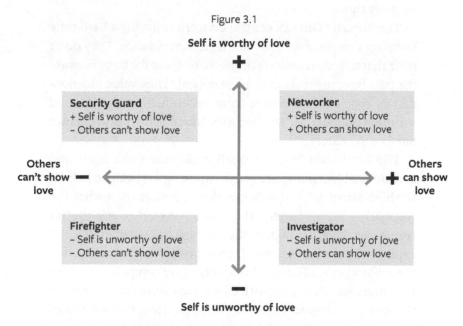

Figure 3.1

Self is worthy of love

Security Guard
+ Self is worthy of love
– Others can't show love

Networker
+ Self is worthy of love
+ Others can show love

Others can't show love

Others can show love

Firefighter
– Self is unworthy of love
– Others can't show love

Investigator
– Self is unworthy of love
+ Others can show love

Self is unworthy of love

Relationship styles recast as work metaphors.

Anxiety and Avoidance: Our Primary Coping Strategies

Another way researchers look at relationship style is by using two dimensions and two common responses to relationship interactions: anxiety and avoidance.

The Firefighter tends to be high in both anxiety and avoidance. They're fraught with anxiety about not being worthy of love and also plagued with avoidance. They seek to keep a perceived safe distance from painful relational interactions.

The Investigator tends to be high in anxiety and lower in avoidance. They are comfortable moving close, but their anxiety leads them to get a bit tangled up. Their central concern is that their relationship partners may not love them as much as they love their partners or that they may have done something to upset them.

The Security Guard's central concern is having a hard time escaping relationship. They are high in avoidance. They don't trust that they can count on others to be there for them because the past has taught them to be skeptical. They value independence, keep a safe distance from relationship partners, and maintain boundaries. The Security Guard is high in avoidance but low in anxiety.

The Networker is low in both avoidance and anxiety and is comfortable moving toward relationships. It can be helpful to think about what the Networker is rather than what the Networker is not. So let's think of a Networker as a master connector. They are high in the courage to be vulnerable and express emotions and needs, high in positive expectations that the self is worthy of love and that others are competent to show love, and high in comfort with closeness/intimacy. However, in the absence of comfortable closeness, our sometimes-virtuous vices—anxiety and avoidance—are present to help us cope.

Lessons in Love

One of the prominent features that differentiates each of the relationship styles is what they have learned about love. Some patterns develop out of convincing experiences that love is available and attainable, and these experiences lay the framework for deep, loving romantic relationships in adulthood. Other styles leave much to be desired, including gaps that need to be filled in order for satisfying romantic relationships to manifest.

The Firefighter: No History of Learning What Love Is

Firefighters are different from all the other relationship styles. Although they have many experiences that nurture a palpable depth of character, there is one thing they lack (in most cases): no one has taught them (during their developmental years) what true love is. They have learned many other lessons but lack the love that is so essential to handling the constant chaotic experiences where there is no safe haven or secure base to help them organize their emotions.

Another thing that sets them apart is their many character-building experiences. They're well-acquainted with sorrow and grief. They have often encountered fearful experiences, lost loved ones, or experienced the fiery trials of trauma. Their important relationship figures may be labeled by others as "difficult" to cope with, or those relationship figures could be absent or unloving, even abusive.

The Firefighter is likely to have faced fires whichever direction they turned. The person the Firefighter needs to go to in order to have their needs met is often the same person who may threaten or hurt them. This puts the Firefighter in a tough situation. If they move toward connection, they risk getting burned; they've faced the blue flames before and have the scars to show for it. The Firefighter may often feel stuck. Their relationship history may have taught them it's dangerous to turn toward their close relationships, so they may have subconsciously grown to believe two painful lies: (1) they aren't worthy of love, and (2) others are unable to love them.

Adaptation has made anxiety and avoidance the Firefighter's close confidants. Firefighters are high both in a tendency to worry about relationships (relationship anxiety) and in a tendency to avoid closeness. They may alternate between these two stances at random. Other times they may face the fire of rejection and move toward the flames. They've experienced so many varying fires that they haven't found one clear strategy that works. They've been forced into trying different strategies and often still feel stuck with an irreconcilable situation. No relationship figures were consistently available to teach them to cope with life's difficulties during their early years, and now they've grown to expect the same chaos from their romantic partners. The Firefighter tends to have many big emotions they are sometimes disconnected from or unaware of.

A teenager in the 1950s, Joey woke up every morning sure of only one thing: if he just worked hard enough or could just be good enough, then he would win his parents' approval. There was only one problem. His strategy failed on days that ended in *y*.

He always got the short end of the stick. If he complained, he was harshly reprimanded. "Don't you dare complain, Joey, or I'll give you something to complain about!" If he heard this once, he heard it a thousand times. Joey strove to not complain, to please his mother, and to do anything to earn love . . . and yet nothing worked.

His brother Brody got all As and earned a nice allowance for his stellar grades. However, when Joey proudly presented his report card of perfect As, his parents said, "Good job, Joey," and though he waited expectantly for the kudos and the cash, he got neither. This made no sense to Joey—but the Firefighter often experiences mixed messages and cannot develop an organized style to deal with them precisely because they don't make sense and the rules are always changing. Instead of cash and kudos, what Joey earned was a lesson—that he was not good enough, no matter how hard he tried.

Time passed, but many things remained the same in Joey's internal world. Joey threw himself into his work in an attempt to earn love; he earned positive feedback and appreciation from his supervisors. He claimed working as a research scientist didn't leave much time for social and family interactions. His loved ones complained that his anxious presence was hard to be around, but he interpreted any complaint as feedback that he had done something wrong or wasn't good enough and, as a result, became fiercely defensive.

Worse for Joey's loved ones, he lacked the reflective function and self-awareness to acknowledge his defensiveness. He was bright and well-respected by his colleagues. He believed since he worked so hard, everyone should be pleased with him. If they weren't, he got angry. He'd flail his arms, holler, scream, rant, and rave.

His first marriage didn't work out.

The path to destruction was paved with Joey's good intentions. I met him when he came to a relationship science marriage retreat desperate to save his second marriage, which was beginning to succumb to the same pattern as the first. The difference was that his second wife told him change was needed. She worried that no matter how much reassurance she gave him, it was never enough to quiet Joey's inner torment. She implored him to come to a relationship styles workshop to begin the journey home to loving connection and relationship security. Joey hesitantly agreed and started his journey toward security.

The Investigator: Learning Inconsistent Loving Patterns

The Investigator has a high capacity to believe that others are competent to show love; however, they struggle to trust that they are lovable. They doubt their value and fear they aren't good enough. They're always on the search for cues that their relationship partner may be onto them as an impostor and are anxious they might move on to greener pastures.

The Investigator moves toward connection, but sometimes their preoccupations and fretting get them tangled up in their relationships.

Barry was an Investigator. He was a passionate man who was unabashedly sentimental. He fell head over heels in love with Lois and always had her on his mind. He also texted her all throughout the day to see what she was doing and to let her know he was thinking of her. Lois had a demanding job as a journalist. She was often in an interview or working on an article. She sometimes didn't bother to charge her phone, and it would die during the day. When Barry didn't receive responses from Lois, he worried that she'd found someone more interesting at work.

For Valentine's Day, Barry bought Lois a phone charger to keep at work. She chuckled and was not impressed. For her birthday, he elevated his pursuit and bought her a very expensive handbag with a built-in phone charger. He hoped that Lois would be able to text him throughout the workday because now her phone wouldn't die.

But Lois sometimes forgot to charge the purse itself, left it in her car, or was just too busy to check her phone. Barry worried that something was wrong with him and kept asking Lois how she felt about him. Lois liked Barry and appreciated his gestures, but eventually it became too much. She was attracted to him but began to sense she couldn't meet his emotional needs. She never felt at peace in the relationship. She was concerned he did not respect her boundaries, and his anxious tendency to hold on when she had to end phone calls or dates was uncomfortable. As time wore on, she realized that despite telling Barry about her concerns he continued with these behaviors, and their relationship had about as much juice as Lois's phone batteries.

Eventually, the inevitability of parting was a reality, and they said their final goodbyes.

The Security Guard: Learning Not to Seek Love

Unlike the Investigator, the Security Guard is high in positive expectations about the self. They believe they're worthy of love (after all, their hard-won independence and competence has taught them the one person they can rely on is themselves); however, they struggle with doubting their relationship partners. They believe their partners aren't able to meet their relational needs. Their relationship history taught them they are on their own. For as long as they can remember, they've been independent and have a strong tendency to move away from relationships and toward other practices, such as sports, collections, work, and hobbies. Their most prominent relationship style feature is the tendency to move away from human connection. This may look different for different Security Guards, but some examples of the Security Guard's narrative for avoiding closeness may include statements to their partner, like: "We don't have to do *everything* together," "I just need some downtime by myself," "I just want to be left alone," and so on. Notice the use of the word *just*. The word *just* serves a role in minimizing the value of their partner in the relationship and minimizing their own feelings and tendency to need anything from the relationship.

Willy was on a date with Gracey. She asked him about his relationship history and his early relationships with his parents. Gracey was a counselor-in-training who was studying relationship science, and she wanted to practice a little on Willy. She was learning so much in her classes and was very interested in dating him too. Wouldn't attachment questions make great conversation starters? So she said, "You mentioned your relationship with your father was supportive. What is your favorite memory of your father being supportive?"

Willy looked away, then replied, "I can't think of one right now."

Patient yet eager to learn more about her date, Gracey said, "No worries, take all the time you need." She looked down as she tried to wait patiently.

Willy shook his head. "All the time I need? We could be here all night long!"

Gracey was a bit shaken; she hadn't expected his response. The next day she told her professor about Willy's responses, and he laughed and told her, "That's a classic response of a [dismissing attachment style] Security Guard!" And the new relationship fell flat before it ever got started.

The Networker: Learning What Love Is and Moving toward It

Simply put, those with the Networker's relationship style know what love is because somewhere along their journey someone *showed them.* Perhaps it was a grandparent who sat with them, read them stories, and delighted in them. Maybe they had a parent who stood up for them when a coach or neighbor did something to hurt them. Or maybe it was a coach or neighbor who took a special interest in them, taught them how to fish, and had meaningful conversations on the way to the local fishing hole.

The Networker understands that love isn't selfish and that it may involve sacrifice and the best interests of the other person. As the Networker navigates romantic relationships, they may need to ask themselves whether they're in love or in "like" with a person. Networkers don't shy away from uncomfortable conversations, but as their relationships deepen and develop, their love for their partners is often comfortable and natural. This is one advantage the Networker has that separates them from the rest of the relationship styles. The Networker not only knows what love is cognitively but also believes and understands it experientially. The Networker was blessed to have someone take the time to teach them what love is.

What's more, the Networker can prove it, meaning they can clearly articulate loving experiences they have had with their partners and early caregivers. If they tell you their relationship with their grandmother was loving growing up and you ask for a specific memory, they can recount a specific episode with freshness and coherence. The Networker is also comfortable expressing valuation of relationships or missing and needing loved ones. They are able to show their feelings and are at ease expressing vulnerable, uncomfortable, and happy feelings without minimizing or exaggerating them. This also makes it easy for their partners to connect with them. The Networker values relationships so much that a breakup or loss of an important loved one causes their world to unravel quickly. As John Bowlby noted, loss is a disorganizing experience.

The Networker isn't carried away by doubt and mistrust. They easily trust others and comfortably move toward them with a positive expectation that they're worthy of love and that others are willing and able to show love. They're less likely to get into a relationship with someone with a less secure style who may not be able to meet their needs.

My college roommate and coworker, Jen, was an easy-breezy Networker. It was exciting to have a front-row seat to her love story. She met Jason at the restaurant where we all worked, and the two hit it off right away. They moved toward connection and began dating. Jen had been seeing someone else before she met Jason, and the two men fought for her for a season. Ultimately, her bond with Jason won out. The two were soon engaged and married, and over two decades later, they're still turning toward each other with a close and affectionate bond. When a coworker of ours died by suicide, Jen and Jason were there to comfort each other. The secure style of the Networker has a relational blueprint that's different from the others—it invites connection.

Measuring Your Relationship Style

How do you determine what your relationship style is? Let's roll up our sleeves and dive into the measurement of relationship styles.

As you think about your particular relationship style and the feedback you get on the quiz, you may find yourself wondering, "Why job titles?" Just as a job serves to meet a person's financial needs—among many other things—a relationship style serves to help a person identify and then meet their emotional and relational needs.

Relationship styles reveal many interpersonal dynamics and offer a glimpse at what is to come (at least indirectly). For example, relationship styles give us insight into our defenses and why we may be more likely to engage in one defensive mechanism, such as suppressing emotional expression,[9] than another, such as exaggerating emotional expression in an effort to cope with emotional pain. Or they could explain why we may share our feelings with a partner when feeling stressed or push them away during challenging times.

> *Relationship styles reveal many interpersonal dynamics and offer a glimpse at what is to come.*

It's important to carefully consider your experiences and thoughts, which can be improved by journaling. This is why in this book I have suggested a journaling prompt, "A Concept to Contemplate," to encourage you to pause and think about your thinking after each chapter.

Identifying Your Relationship Style

There are several different assessments available, and they measure relationship styles in different ways. For example, the Adult Attachment Interview (AAI) is an interview that typically takes about an hour. It's then transcribed verbatim and coded. The AAI is a robust, valid, and reliable test for measuring one's relationship style and can predict the relationship style of a child many years later based on an interview of their mother when they were in the womb! Simply put, the AAI gives careful analysis of one's state of mind about early relationships based on how a person tells their relationship story.

Relationship Styles Test (Short Form)

Each of the items that follow relate to how you feel in relationships that are emotionally intimate. Please answer each prompt with respect to how you generally experience close relationship partners.[10] The purpose of this test is to help you understand your relationship style as you connect in romantic relationships. This survey is best taken privately, though you may discuss your results with your partner later.

Directions: Please first read the scenario in step 1 and then answer the questions in step 2. If you would like to take the survey privately, record your answers elsewhere.

On items relating to romantic relationships, please rate your current relationship. If you are currently single, please rate your most recent relationship. If you have not been in a relationship, please rate the response you most identify with. For each item, please select the response that is *most true*.

Step 1: Activate Your Relationship System with a Story

Imagine you have been watching a TV show with your romantic partner. The series is about a young woman named Sarah who is on a quest to find love. Sarah has an opportunity to date several people and find her match. She has had her heart broken in the past by a boyfriend who treated her poorly, and she is trying to open her heart and find someone who will love her and whom she can love in return.

Sarah lives on the East Coast and works full-time as an elementary school teacher. She has spent time by the ocean because it brought her peace and comfort after her breakup. Sarah meets Matt on the second episode of the program. He is an EMT, he loves to help people, and he has also found that spending time near the water helps him de-stress. On their first date, Matt and Sarah go to a sea turtle preserve, try swimming with sea turtles, and have a picnic and romantic walk on the beach. It is like love at first sight! The two feel at ease together. It's as if they have known each other all their lives, even though they've just met. After a few dates, Matt professes his love to Sarah and gives her a promise ring before telling her he is saving up for an engagement ring.

You and your date find you can relate to these characters; you like both of them and are rooting for them to ride off into the sunset together. However, in tonight's episode, while they are riding horses on the beach, Matt is shaken off his horse and falls headfirst onto the sand. He is unresponsive, and Sarah is frantic as she calls 911. The ambulance comes and takes them to the hospital, where it is determined Matt is in a coma. Sarah stays by his side, praying for him to wake up. She is crying and saying, "Matt, please don't leave me. I love you too. I did not get a chance to say it back when you first told me, but I *must* tell you I love you. Don't go! Please wake up!"

The purpose of reading this story is to activate your relationship system. (As an alternative, you can also watch a clip from *Titanic* where the lovers are separated.) If you imagined yourself in Sarah's shoes and are wondering if Sarah's prayer will be answered and Matt will wake up, or if he will be gone forever and she will have to say goodbye, *your relationship system is likely activated*. This should help you access the thoughts associated with your relationship system and answer the questions most accurately to access your relationship blueprint.

Step 2: Answer the Following Questions

Please select the answer that is most true for you in the context of your romantic relationship (with a past or present romantic partner).

1. When I feel sad, I _____.
   A. Get overwhelmed and am not sure what to do. I want to get away from my partner and the situation, or I blame myself or my partner.
   B. Get really discouraged and try to talk with my partner—but I get upset with them for making it worse. I tell myself I should've known something bad would happen and feel upset. I think about how they seem to always make things worse and dwell on this.
   C. Just try to ignore it and think about something else.
   D. Lean into my sadness, reflect on it, and go to my partner and share my feelings. I often let my partner comfort me with a hug, a listening ear, or an encouraging word, and then I feel closer to them and affectionate toward them.

2. When I feel angry, I _____.
   A. Don't know whether or not to talk to my partner about my feelings. I get overwhelmed by the anger and get frustrated by the discussion. Sometimes I just want to avoid talking to them, but I wonder if I should and then I feel stuck.
   B. Get exasperated and wish I could share my feelings with my partner, but I get frustrated when they do

not seem to understand. Or I worry they may not love me or accept me if they really knew me.

C. Avoid talking with my partner and don't think about my feelings.

D. Allow myself to lean into the anger and understand what it is telling me. Then I share my feelings with my partner. I try to vent in a way that does not hurt their feelings but gives me a chance to express my concerns, and then I feel relieved and heard.

3. When I feel anxious, I _____.

A. Feel stuck and unsure whether I should go to my partner or whether that will make it worse. I sometimes feel like I should avoid talking with them and ignore the feeling, and at other times I feel overwhelmed and worried. I may engage in a nonproductive discussion with my partner.

B. Worry a lot and sometimes wait until it gets to be too much and I can't take it anymore before I mention it to my partner. Then I am really upset and sometimes that gets them upset, and talking seems to make it worse.

C. Try to minimize any anxious thoughts or feelings and deal with them on my own and avoid sharing them with my partner.

D. Allow myself to lean into the anxiety and really feel it, then I share my worries with my partner as soon as they come up. I feel relief just from sharing the burden, and I feel closer to my partner.

4. Please rate the following statements on a scale from 1 to 7, where 1 is strongly disagree and 7 is strongly agree:

_____ A. I am worried my partner might stop loving me.

_____ B. I am scared that I love my partner much more than they love me.

_____ C. I do not like it when my partner tries to get too close.

_____ D. I prefer to keep my emotions in check rather than disclose them.

5. If my partner was watching a movie and said the main character was very attractive, I would feel
_____.

A. Overwhelmed by a mix of emotions such as jealousy, anxiety, or the desire to withdraw. I would blame myself or others and avoid talking about it, ruminate on it, and/or start a nonproductive discussion.

B. Anxious my partner may not really love me and begin comparing myself to the main character. I may worry about my partner leaving me.

C. Like avoiding the comments or changing the subject.

D. A slight twinge of anxiety that I may not be attractive or good enough, but the feeling would not linger.

6. Which of the following responses best communicates *the type of response* you would have to the prompt below. (Note: Your actual memories and situation may differ but identify the item that best describes the way you think through or process thoughts, feelings,

or memories that come up related to your romantic relationships.)

Prompt: *You used the word* challenging *to describe your relationship with your partner; please indicate a specific memory that illustrates how that relationship was challenging.*

A. My relationship with my partner was challenging because they would keep me waiting for a text reply. While I waited, I would feel so anxious that something happened to them, I'd try to go see them in person or I'd text their friends to make sure they were OK. Other times I felt frustrated and thought about just deleting their number or blocking them so I wouldn't have to see their name on my phone.

B. My relationship with my partner was challenging because they kept me waiting a week after our first several dates, causing me to feel anxious and frustrated. I kept analyzing the dates and thinking about the reasons they may not have liked me. And even now, they still have not contacted me to schedule our next date, and I have no clue what the plan is or when we will get together again, and so I am worried about it . . .

C. My relationship with my partner was challenging because a relationship can be challenging. There are much more interesting things to talk about, like the weather.

D. My relationship with my partner was challenging because after our first date, they waited nearly a week to text me, and the waiting was hard because I really liked them and thought they did not like me.

7. Please select which of the following items best represents your approach to romantic relationships:

A. I feel uncomfortable being vulnerable with romantic partners. I feel a mixture of anxiety and avoidance. At times I feel anxious being close with others, and at other times I want to avoid closeness with them.

B. I value being close to others but feel anxious that they may not want to be close because of something in me. I also feel unworthy of their support and anxious when they want to depend on me. If I am really honest, I am afraid that they may not love me as much as I love them.

C. I value being independent and avoid depending on others in close relationships. I also prefer to minimize my expression of emotions toward romantic partners or close friends and prefer not to be depended on by others or have others depend on me.

D. I feel comfortable with being close with and vulnerable with romantic partners, and I also feel at ease depending on others and having them depend on me emotionally.

Step 3: Calculate Your Results

Scoring Instructions: Among the seven questions above, items 1 and 2 measure anxiety, items 3 and 4 measure avoidance, items 5 and 6 measure state of mind related to romantic relationship styles, and item 7 measures your approach to emotion in the context of relationship. Although you may relate to more than one style, the style that shows up the most in your responses is your primary romantic relationship style.

Transfer your answers here or to your journal:

1. _____   5. _____
2. _____   6. _____
3. _____   7. _____
4. A. _____
   B. _____
   C. _____
   D. _____

For items 1 through 3, if you answered:

- Mostly As = Firefighter
- Mostly Bs = Investigator
- Mostly Cs = Security Guard
- Mostly Ds = Networker

For item 4, letters A and B measure anxiety, and letters C and D measure avoidance:

- If you scored 1–3 on anxiety and 1–3 on avoidance, you are likely a Networker.
- If you scored 1–3 on anxiety and a 6 or above on avoidance, you are likely a Security Guard.
- If you scored 5–7 on anxiety and 1–3 on avoidance, you are likely an Investigator.
- If you scored 5 or above on both anxiety and avoidance, you may be a Firefighter.

For items 5 through 7, if you answered:

- Mostly As = Firefighter
- Mostly Bs = Investigator
- Mostly Cs = Security Guard
- Mostly Ds = Networker

My primary relationship style is likely the _____.

Does this information surprise you? I suspect it doesn't. The next four chapters will give you more information on each relationship style and put you on the path to better relationships with your loved ones. If you want even more confirmation and information about identifying your style, please visit my website, DrAnitaKuhnley.com.

KEY TAKEAWAYS

- The way you approach relationships is similar to the way you approach feelings.
- There are several different ways to measure your relationship style. The Relationship Styles Test (Short Form) integrates components of various measurement methods and expert reviews to provide an abbreviated version of a self-report instrument.
- Reading the story before the test or watching a clip from *Titanic* that activates the relationship system can increase accuracy in answering the test questions. It is best to answer the questions as honestly as possible, as denial cures nothing.

A CONCEPT TO CONTEMPLATE

Did taking the test give you any aha moments about yourself or your relationships? This is a great time to take out your journal to record these and other eureka moments you have when you notice your relational blueprints informing your dating life, your marriage, or your other relationships. Part of the journey toward optimizing your relationship style involves increasing self-awareness, so this will help propel you forward. May God grant you insight.

> *I pray that the eyes of your heart may be enlightened in order that you may know the hope to which he has called you, the riches of his glorious inheritance in his holy people, and his incomparably great power for us who believe.*
>
> *Ephesians 1:18–19*

4

The Firefighter

In the movie *As Good as It Gets*, Jack Nicholson plays Melvin, a romance novelist with obsessive-compulsive disorder and a variety of eccentric personality quirks. He eats breakfast at the same diner every day and is waited on by Carol, the only server who can tolerate his behavior, played by Helen Hunt. He also avoids cracks in the sidewalk, uses a new bar of soap every time he washes his hands, and refuses to be interrupted, no matter the issue. And yet, unbeknownst to him, he is on an unlikely journey to find love.

Eventually, Melvin finds himself on a trip with unlikely companions: his neighbor Simon and his favorite server, Carol. The three of them are all single, and each has been dealt a unique set of challenges in life: Carol is caring for her chronically ill son, Simon has significant injuries from a robbery, and Melvin is, well, difficult. Melvin reflects on their stories saying,

Some of us have great stories. Pretty stories that take place at lakes with boats and friends and noodle salad. Just no one in this car. But

a lot of people, that's their story. Good times. Noodle salad. What
makes it so hard is not that you had it bad, but that you're pissed
that so many others had it good.[1]

Melvin highlights the struggle of the Firefighter: their story
is often one of facing many adversities and challenges. It may
not be a story of lighthearted romantic walks in the park; the
Firefighter finds it hard to maintain a sense of humor and balance in sharing their story. Life can be a challenge. Let's look
at a more specific example of one Firefighter's story.

A Look at Firefighters: Anne

An orphan named Anne was sent to Green Gables, where
aging brother and sister, Matthew and Marilla Cuthbert, had
requested and expected a boy to work on their farm. So Anne's
circumstance was already awkward and not the adoption she
had dreamed of. Then one day Marilla asked Anne to put away
her shawl and broach, a precious heirloom of her grandmother's
that Anne had overtly admired.

Later, Marilla went in search of the broach and panicked
when she did not see it on the chair where Anne had placed
the shawl. Outraged, she confronted Anne, demanding that the
girl confess to stealing the broach or she'd send her back to the
orphanage. Anne was at first frozen in fear by Marilla's threats;
she dreaded the thought of returning to the traumatic place.
So she made up a vivid story of how she dropped the broach
in a well. Marilla didn't believe a word of it and banished Anne
back to the orphanage.

Anne was untalkative and detached as she departed from
Green Gables. It was completely out of character for Anne to be
silent, as she was usually an extroverted, voracious talker, but
the entire ride to the train station, she sat in the horse-drawn
carriage without uttering a word.

Shortly after her departure, Marilla discovered that the broach had fallen into a crevice between the chair's cushions. She ran down the steps, calling out to Matthew who was working outside, and pleaded with him to go and find Anne.

After much searching, Matthew finally found her at the train station, selling made-up stories to earn her train fare. She was telling a story to several ladies when Matthew approached her. She ignored him, but he implored Anne to come home. She told him she wasn't going to go with him just so they could banish her again whenever they felt like it.

A High-Functioning Firefighter

Anne never met her biological parents. She lost them before she had a chance to know them. She also went through abuse and trauma at the hands of one of her foster families. She was chronically finding fires to put out, and as a result, she became an excellent Firefighter. Whether they were "fires" that Anne started or they stemmed from another's misadventure, she perpetually found herself getting burned. Anne doubted Marilla and Matthew's capacity to love her *and* her capacity to be loved by them. Anne was clearly angry with Matthew and Marilla and blamed them for thinking she was a thief and for sending her away.

Eventually, Marilla and Matthew sought to rectify the harm done. They became more loving toward Anne, and they all grew and developed through their relationship. Sometime later, the Cuthberts officially adopted Anne into their family by inviting her to sign her name in their family Bible.

Anne's an example of a high-functioning Firefighter who is on a journey of becoming more self-aware and secure. She values relationships with her best friend, her new parents, and her love interest. Through stories, she is able to express her thoughts and fears about her red hair, her name, and other aspects of herself she finds unlovable. Trauma researchers know that when people have a chance to share their story with loved ones or a therapist right after a traumatic experience, they are less likely to have severe PTSD symptoms later and less likely to have long-term suffering. Anne's journaling, writing, talking to herself, and active imagination likely helped her enhance her functioning within her relationship style blueprint.

Anne eventually learned to integrate those fires into her story in a meaningful way. When her relationship system was activated by stress, it took longer for her to calm down and feel safe, but she continued to cultivate her capacity to use the skills at her disposal—her vivid imagination, storytelling capabilities, poetic speech, and hopeful outlook—to facilitate her coping and enhance her functioning.

Given the chronic stress most Firefighters face, those who have experienced trauma may experience post-traumatic stress disorder (PTSD) and are more likely to struggle with a cluster of symptoms that are linked with hyperarousal (where the body moves into a state of high alert and is on the lookout for danger),[2] externalizing behaviors (clinical parlance for irritability and outbursts of anger), and avoidance behaviors that include numbing sensations or dissociative behaviors (where the mind goes somewhere else and disconnects from bodily sensations).

The Firefighter's Origin Story

As a child, the Firefighter often encountered chaotic environments and absent or abusive caregivers. Inherently, these encounters were disorganizing. This makes it difficult for the adult Firefighter to find their home in the heart of another and challenging to think of themselves as lovable.

There is a pretty wide range of clinical terminology when it comes to categorizing some relationship styles. Those who encountered frightening experiences, for example, have not developed an organized blueprint for dealing with early relationships and are often described as having a relationship style that is *disorganized* or *fearful avoidant*. There is a similar category called *unresolved* that includes individuals who experienced abuse and loss that is yet to be reconciled into a coherent autobiographical narrative. Firefighters' encounters with trauma, loss, mixed signals, or chaotic experiences often yield one of three types of Firefighter profiles.

Overwhelmed Due to Loss

One type of Firefighter has experienced the pain of loss and has still not come to terms with it. It's typically the loss of a caregiver or a partner. In romantic attachment, this could invoke jealousy and feelings of sadness due to losing a romantic partner to a rival, whether real or imagined.[3] For people with abusive or harsh relationship figures in their past, even the loss of a pet or the loss of a job or change in situation can be unsettling and lead to internal disorganization.

In *Anne of Green Gables*, Anne says, "I'm sorry because this drive has been so pleasant, and I am always sorry when pleasant things end. Still, something pleasanter may come afterward, but you can never be sure. And it is so often the case that it isn't pleasanter. That has been my experience anyhow."[4] Despite how pleasant or unpleasant a relationship is deemed, saying our final goodbyes is always disorganizing.

Unsure Due to a History of Mixed Signals

Children need to know if they can approach their caregiver to receive comfort or nurturance and if it is safe and appropriate to do so. As children, some Firefighters weren't clear whether it was safe to approach their safe haven or secure base; at times, it could even be dangerous, yet that was the only set of caregivers they had. They faced an irreconcilable situation, and in adulthood, they may chaotically and haphazardly shift back and forth between Security Guard strategies and Investigator strategies in a disorganized manner.[5]

As adults, some Firefighters tend to feel stuck and not quite sure how to respond to relational situations they face with partners. Perhaps they have felt stuck in what counselors call a double bind where there is a negative consequence to whatever decision is made. There may be some incongruent messaging in all relationships, but in some Firefighters' experience, inconsistency was the primary distinguishing feature of their relationships. This often led them to feel perpetually stuck, invalidated, and not sure how to respond well. The Firefighter also tends to struggle with self-regulation and, at times, may feel like their relationships and emotions are spiraling out of control. In adult romantic relationships, partners take turns serving as one another's safe haven and secure base. The Firefighter may feel uncomfortable with both of these roles and both the giving and receiving of support. They may have a disorganized response to interpersonal relationships.

Children need to know if they can approach their caregiver to receive comfort or nurturance.

Chronically Putting Out Fires Due to Abuse

It is important to remember that Firefighters have faced trauma. They've been burned by the flames of painful interpersonal relationships. Ironically, it's often abuse at the hands of the people they expected to love them most—such as parents, caregivers, or romantic partners. When they resolve this abuse, they often feel more secure in their relationship style and experience less relationship anxiety, less avoidance, and/or more comfort with closeness. Ultimately, through much work in therapy or personal work such as journaling and bibliotherapy, a Firefighter may transform to higher levels of functioning with a more structured style.

The Firefighter's Relationship Blueprint

Like an architect's blueprint guides the process of building a home, a relationship blueprint is an internal guide for how we build (or struggle to build) relationships. This looks different for each of the relationship styles. The Firefighter's blueprint is a cautionary tale analyzing all the potential fire hazards along the way. Not only are Firefighters good at finding relational challenges; they also tend to be drawn to individuals who have the same dysregulated tendencies they encountered in their early days. Their relationship blueprint often leaves them fixated on the possible painful challenges they want to avoid in the relationship and unable to build romantic relationships smoothly.

Our relationship blueprints (or internal working models) are framed by the answers to two pressing ponderings of our hearts.

Am I worthy of love? The answer involves considering what conclusions I can draw about my worthiness of love based on my experiences with early caregivers and the capacity of others to love and be available to me.

Can others be counted on to love me? Our expectations inform this answer—specifically our expectations about what we can come to expect from our important relationship figures in terms of whether they will be reliable and available to be our safe haven during times of stress.

Many Firefighters' early contact with caregivers was often more than deficient nurturing—it was an encounter with danger. They were perpetually in crisis mode; there was always a fire to put out. In adulthood, some find themselves in frightening or stressful romantic relationships where they are constantly "walking on eggshells."

The Firefighter must contend with a compound relational challenge, facing both the problems of Investigators (see chap. 5) and Security Guards (see chap. 6), leaving them with a mixture of fearfulness like the Investigator and avoidant tendencies like the Security Guard.

The Firefighters' misadventures leave them with hope-crushing conclusions, which are often beyond their conscious awareness. Answers to the two important questions shared above look something like this (though these responses may be subconscious):

Am I worthy of love? "I am unworthy of love. My most important relationship figures and early caregivers didn't find me lovable; they must be right. They provided inconsistent care, were absent, or even harmed me during my developmental years. I sometimes *think* I'm worthy of love, but most of the time I don't *feel* worthy of love, and my experiences have taught me that I am not. Even if I tell myself I am, there is a dissonance, and it is hard to truly believe it emotionally." (High-functioning Firefighters are self-aware and are doing the work to resolve the dissonance, though it is far from easy.)

Can others be counted on to love me? The Firefighter again comes up dry, and the conclusion is the same. Others cannot be counted on for love. Worse, they're often abusive or neglectful. Their relationship blueprint silently echoes the lonely internal story, "I cannot count on others to care for me. In my past experiences, I have not been able to count on anyone to be there for me consistently, so it is hard to trust in the context of romantic relationships."

Ouch. As you can imagine, having a negative response to both important questions leaves the Firefighter feeling like toast that's burnt on both sides of the bread. Recovering from fighting fires is a long journey, but the good news is even the Firefighter who has been dealt the cards of extreme trauma or loss isn't stuck. God always has a plan, and life offers new opportunities to find and create a secure base (see chap. 8).

Understanding the Firefighter

The Firefighter has to fight fires on both sides of the fence—they have to cope with the fear or anger that fuels the preoccupation of the Investigator and the tendency of the Security Guard to push people away and look for an escape route.

These fearful avoidant tendencies often lead the Firefighter to find deep drama all throughout their journey, even in the little moments. Their bids for connection may have failed during childhood or been met with intense danger, so in adulthood, Firefighters may lean toward avoidance and may be slow to pursue and initiate. As they hesitate, they may miss opportunities for love or may send their would-be partner mixed signals. The Firefighter may have an enormous desire for love but often feels like their world is unraveling when they get into close relationships. Likewise, their anxiety may prompt them to barrel toward the pursuit of their love interest like a husband whose wife's water just broke flying out of the driveway on two wheels.

Firefighters develop a nonlinear narrative that includes relational detours away from connection and routes to connection that circle endlessly, making it doubly challenging to connect. The Firefighter needs reassurance, but if they are low-functioning and not working on self-awareness or introspection, even the most emotionally intelligent partner is unlikely to be able to help them be present in a healing relationship. That said, if the Firefighter leans into the discomfort and moves toward yeses in their relational blueprints, they may find a new narrative—that they have a lot of love to give.

Emotions and the Firefighter

In addition to developing a blueprint with respect to relationship expectations, early experiences also help the Firefighter develop a blueprint that guides their responses to emotions. The Firefighter does not have an organized approach to feelings. Like the Security Guard, they may seek to deactivate their emotions and dismiss, minimize, or discount their emotional experiences. This minimization may lead to them being out of touch with their emotions. At other times, they may get overwhelmed by emotional experiences and tend to exaggerate them, be emotionally flooded, and struggle to engage in emotionally intelligent practices, such as using emotions to spark thought or remaining open to an emotion without exaggerating it or minimizing the emotion. They may also engage in a haphazard and chaotic oscillation between these two different approaches to emotion and struggle with managing emotions in an organized way.

One of the most important factors that determines the outcome of a couple's conflict-related discussion of a perpetual problem is one partner (often the wife or girlfriend) starting the discussion with a soft and gentle tone. Relationship researchers call this a soft start-up.[6] Conversely, if a conversation begins out of the gate with a harsh tone, including critical remarks and/or sarcasm, this is considered a harsh start-up.[7] You can predict how the conversation (or relationship) will end based on how it begins. A harsh start-up may be tougher for the Firefighter to avoid due to their difficulty with managing emotions, so it may be beneficial for Firefighters to learn to put a pin in it or take a break to disengage—ideally a minimum of twenty minutes—until they can return with a gentle and kind start-up.

The Brain Science of the Firefighter's Style

The front part of the brain is called the prefrontal cortex (PFC). It's the executive command center or "boss in your brain" that keeps you on task.[8] When the PFC is working well, you are likely to act more empathically toward your partner. When the PFC is functioning well, it assists you with being patient with your partner and makes you more goal-oriented.

The PFC modulates what happens in the subcortical parts of the brain, like the brain stem and limbic area.

If you have the Firefighter's style and someone cuts you off in traffic, you sense you've been slighted. Your brain will start firing off—the alarm will sound that the situation isn't safe. Of course, this is very helpful if you're walking beside a lake in Florida and a gator approaches you—you need to get away fast. However, your sympathetic nervous system doesn't know the difference between a hungry gator and a cranky partner; an alarm bell is an alarm bell.

So, if you're exposed to a situation where your partner criticizes you and it triggers unresolved trauma, you may find your PFC isn't as accessible. Your limbic system and the parts of your brain associated with emotional memories are more active. You may become more reactive and feel like your brain is shutting down. Perhaps part of you wants to retreat and curl up under the covers and cry, part of you wants to remain present and advocate for yourself, and another part of you just wants to run away and leave the relationship altogether. You may find that you become more rigid in your responses, unable to connect or be present with your partner.[9] You may become flooded with painful emotions such as fear or rage. Researchers call this *bottom-up processing, low mode,* or *low road.*[10]

If a person has unresolved struggles, they're more vulnerable to spending time on the low road. When someone has a knee-jerk reaction, such as yelling at others in traffic or snapping at their partner for something minor, they may be experiencing this type of bottom-up processing that makes it more difficult to respond with forethought and empathy.

When a person is on the low road, the PFC doesn't inhibit the limbic system from taking over. Anything can happen at this point. It's a trauma response in which a person goes into fight, flight, freeze, or fawn mode. Dr. Dan Siegel says people are capable of doing or saying horrible things that don't align with their values when on the low road.[11] On the low road, a person's attachment system is activated, and they don't feel safe.

How long does it take to return to the high road? This depends on several factors. If we don't take the time to pursue healing from our past struggles, the process is circuitous. When we take time to reflect and make meaning of our experiences, we become more resilient and thoughtful in our responses.[12] The more we work to understand our relationship style and our relationship blueprint, as well as the triggers that elevate our relationship anxiety and relationship avoidance, the more high-functioning our relationship style will become and the easier it will become to stay regulated and shift to the high road. People with more secure styles tend to be high in a process called *metacognitive monitoring* in which they think about their thinking. Therapists are always trying to encourage and promote this type of self-awareness by encouraging metacognition. In some studies, as the ability to think about thinking in real time went up, relationship anxiety went down.[13] So, perhaps in cases when our thoughts are spiraling and we feel emotionally overwhelmed, instead of using the motivational self-talk script "keep calm and carry on," it would be more helpful to say, "In order to keep calm, take a step back and think about your thinking."

> *When we take time to reflect and make meaning of our experiences, we become more resilient and thoughtful in our responses.*

If we're consciously aware that we may get stuck on unhelpful thoughts, it may indicate that our brain's gearshift—the anterior cingulate gyrus—is stuck. In these cases, Dr. Daniel Amen, a child and adult psychiatrist, suggests we engage in a practice called *thought stopping*. In this practice, we try to realize that our brain's gearshift is stuck. We can attempt to bring the PFC back online by saying to ourselves, *Stop. This is just my anterior cingulate gyrus getting stuck!*[14]

Those with the Firefighter style are vulnerable to the low road because they've experienced difficult relational journeys, trauma that hasn't been resolved, or grief that hasn't been healed. If you or your partner are often disposed to the low road, it is more likely that your child (or any future children) will develop an insecure relationship style. If you are a Firefighter, you may find that you love your partner very much but you struggle to love them very well.

Loving the Firefighter

If you're a Firefighter or if you love a Firefighter, counseling and personal development are your friends. Your future self will thank you for investing in therapy and self-development exercises.

Some Strategies to Keep in Mind to Love Your Firefighter Well

- Carry your QTIP—yes, let the little white ear cleaner be a reminder of the acronym it can represent—Quit Taking It Personally. Do not take their challenges in managing moods personally. In other words, if you can remember that the seeming rejection isn't about you but about the Firefighter's own discomfort and pain, their distancing may be less painful.

- Ask them how they are feeling and how their heart is, and then listen with more than your ears.[15]

- Remain inquisitive and ask them about their needs to "give them permission" to have needs of their own. (They may have had past relationships where their needs were treated as if they did not matter.)

- Be generous with reassurance. Try to reassure your partner that you love them. When you request a change or share a complaint, remind them you love them just the way they are, and tell them your request is for the good of *the relationship* rather than a rejection of *them*.
- Share your feelings first. When appropriate, it may help the Firefighter get in touch with their own feelings.
- When possible, share your positive emotional experiences in the moment. For example: "Ah, the feeling of this warm mug in my hands is comforting and soothing. I can feel the hot cocoa warming me from the inside out."
- Share positive feedback and feelings with your partner. If you think your partner looks good, tell them. If you enjoyed your time together, don't keep it a secret. Research has revealed stable successful couples tend to have a positive emotional climate. Think of these positive interactions like coins in your relationship bank account. Each one adds a penny to the account, while each criticism (or other negative interaction) deducts a nickel. Stable couples keep those pennies flowing to stay in the relational black.[16]
- Do your best to use a soft start-up when discussing conflict, and encourage that use by your partner. For example: "Can we talk about your concerns over a cup of coffee at the table, so I can fully focus on what you're saying? That will give us a surface to outline some solutions if needed."
- Try "speaking" all five of the love languages and exercise patience. It may take your partner a while before they feel loved by you.
- Ask your partner about their triggers, but be careful not to use those vulnerabilities against them (this would be

a betrayal of trust). Be sensitive and navigate around the triggers they share with you.

• Give the gift of empathy whenever possible.

The Gift of Empathy

If you love a Firefighter, there's no hack or fast lane to healing. Your Firefighter needs patience and empathy. If empathy isn't your strong suit, here are three shelf-worthy book recommendations for you: *Feeling Good Together* by David Burns, *Loving What Is* by Byron Katie, and my previous book, *The Mister Rogers Effect* (especially "Secret 5").

Empathy is not sympathy. Sympathy says, "I'm sorry for your loss," while empathy says, "It must feel painful to have lost your pet who was such an important part of your family and who was an integral part of your day-to-day life for so many years. Help me understand how you're coping."

Giving the gift of empathy combined with expressions of care may sound like, "I admire the way you've overcome the challenges you faced during your childhood and the way you chose to respond to the circumstances that were out of your control. Help me understand what it's like when you face people who've hurt you so deeply in the past."

Positive Feedback Your Firefighter Can Use

Taking time to acknowledge the good experiences in our lives and meditating on them can magnify those things and the happiness-boosting effects they have. Having the capacity to savor life's positive experiences is considered one of the most crucial ingredients in the recipe of happiness (in or out of romantic relationships).[17] If you focus on everything that's wrong in your relationship with a Firefighter, you will magnify problems until you're looking at life through the blue lens of depression. One quick path to breakup and divorce is talking and thinking about everything your partner does that you don't like. However, a pathway to relationship longevity is having eyes to see the good your partner does *that you do like* and not being a secret admirer but rather a genuine and effusive expressor. For example:

- "Wow, sweetie, you look very handsome in that tie. Thank you for dressing up."
- "I just wanted to say I really respect how hard you work to take care of us. It means a lot to me."
- "My love, you look beautiful in that dress! Va-voom!"
- "Thanks for taking out the trash today, honey. I really appreciate your taking care of that."

Each positive expression is another deposit improving the emotional tone of the relationship. We now know, courtesy of what relationship research has revealed, that the masters of marriage (when compared to what researchers call the "disasters of marriage") seem to win in the small things.[18] They succeed at creating a five-to-one ratio: five positive interactions for every one negative. The couples called the "disasters of marriage" have a much lower ratio.

Little things become big things over time. These principles are relevant to all couples, but they are especially important for the Firefighter since their relationships have had many roadblocks and the management of emotion is an added obstacle. Firefighters have the disadvantage of not having memories of sensitive and responsive caregivers that they can imagine and internalize.

Interventions

If your partner isn't open to counseling, consider couples' enrichment retreats. If your partner is willing to go to either, willingness to join in without complaint will serve you both well. But be aware that you have a wonderful challenge ahead. Your Firefighter may literally be willing to walk through fire to keep your relationship afloat. Their history may not have included many satisfying relationships, so the ones they have are hard-won and become even more precious. Firefighters feel intensely and sometimes fluctuate from love to hate or from a pleasant mood to an angry mood, so I suggest keeping the QTIP mantra in your back pocket.

Engaging in personal counseling and garnering support can be helpful, and having other nurturing relationships—whether from your church, a trusted counselor, or understanding and reassuring friendships—can help you feel fulfilled and relieve the pressure from depending on your partner to meet needs in ways they do not have the resources to do.

Be a Safe Haven and a Secure Launching Pad

Remember that an attachment figure or a secure relationship partner serves as a safe haven at times. It's wise to make it our business to find out what helps our partners feel safe and then become a pro at that. Did your partner have a special relationship with their grandfather that they found comforting? Or maybe they had a best friend who was there for them during some rough patches. You can help your partner feel safe by showing an interest in that connection with their friend or grandparent. Become curious and have a sense of awe and wonder as you listen to them recount stories of special memories.

Validate Feelings

It isn't uncommon for a Firefighter to be emotionally unavailable, disconnected, or emotionally overwhelmed. Like relationships, emotions have been tough for them to manage given the misadventures of their journey. You can help by not taking it personally and by validating emotions.

I want to take a moment to review a key emotional intelligence principle: feelings are mentionable and manageable.[19] If your partner can mention and process their feelings, their emotions become easier to manage. However, this may be a new process for them. Often, Firefighters grew up in atmospheres that didn't welcome expression, so their emotions will be pent-up like a fully wound jack-in-the-box. If you're able to provide a safe space for your partner to share those big feelings and validate them through active listening, this practice can encourage them to feel comfortable expressing their emotions and cultivating emotional intimacy.

Communicate Your Needs

Your Firefighter is likely interested in pleasing you and loving you well, but that will not come naturally. Difficulty in expressing their emotions and needs may manifest in passive-aggressive tendencies or submissive hostility. They may be hanging out in Shouldville, subscribing to the belief that you should already know all of their needs and feelings without them having to explain or express anything. To help, you can stay in Realville where if you want or need something you often have to ask. And don't forget your QTIP. Modeling emotional expression and requesting it from your partner can be a great help as well.

Though it requires vulnerability and strength, it is helpful to communicate about your needs directly so you're ready to engage and explore together. If you have one of the other relationship styles, this direct communication may be more comfortable for you. Perhaps you can help your partner on their journey of making the most of their relationship style. As they see you model communicating your needs, they may find it easier to communicate their own.

You may be asking, "What if I'm a Firefighter too?" Remember, denial heals nothing. If you're asking whether you have this style, congratulations; your willingness to self-reflect is a feather in your cap. Many people lack the willingness and awareness to consider their relationship style. Counselors often remark that it isn't the people in counseling you have to worry about. Those people know they have areas to develop and are actively working on them. It's the people who think the problems are everyone else's fault that

Remember, denial heals nothing.

you really need to be concerned with. Self-awareness and the capacity to *think about your thinking* are characteristics associated with relationship security. By compassionately reflecting on your Firefighter partner's tendencies, or your own, you're on your way to developing a higher-functioning relationship style and enhancing your relationship security.

There are several tools the Firefighter and/or the Firefighter's partner can add to their personal development tool kit to help fine-tune their relationship style.

- Journal to make feelings mentionable and manageable. Emotion dysregulation may be a problem.
- Use a feeling wheel (a pie chart available at my website) to identify emotions. Feeling faces display emotions in picture form and are a child-friendly tool.
- Notice the Firefighter's tendency toward projective identification and redirect it. Projective identification is what therapists often refer to when we're so uncomfortable with our emotions that we use another person as a receptacle, projecting our emotions onto them and creating pressure to the point that the other person projects or contains the unwanted emotion.
- Try dialectical behavioral therapy (DBT) skills training. DBT involves combining opposite (dialectical) factors such as acceptance (*who I am right now is OK*) with the

95

desire for change (*I want to improve*). DBT helps clients identify triggers that lead to feeling emotionally over-whelmed and match triggers with a specific protocol of coping mechanisms that may help. This training proto-col is often used in counseling or group counseling for people who struggle to manage their emotions. Since re-lationships serve a regulatory function, it isn't a surprise that it may also be helpful for those with interpersonal injuries or traumas to regulate their emotions and orga-nize their feelings.

- Identify a safe haven. What helps you feel safe? If you don't have a relationship partner or a family, consider your relationship with God, a friend, or a mentor. Visual-ize someone who has loved you into being who you are and think of them when you need to "go to your safe space."

- Pets can serve an emotion-regulation function and some people find that, because their anxiety about negative experiences in relationship with people is too high, it is easier to relate to a pet. If you don't have a pet, you can experience a similar calming and comforting effect by visualizing an animal you would enjoy petting—whether a cat, dog, horse, or other animal.

- Keep a journal in which you name your emotions and the connections between thoughts, feelings, and behaviors.

- Work with a counselor or a safe professional to process loss, abuse, or trauma.

Benefits of the Firefighter's Style

The Firefighter's fire hose wasn't just an instrument to shield them from the dangerous relationship figures in early life; it also became an instrument that repelled the pleasant flames of romantic love. But if they can learn to wield it carefully, it can become a tool for good use.

The Firefighter has lived in crisis mode, and they learned to survive. When you need someone to act quickly in a crisis, the Firefighter can process information quickly and take action. In some cases when they're triggered, the Firefighter's behaviors become more rigid. Their protective strategies make great servants but poor masters. But when their PFC comes back online, they have the flexibility to engage in a wide range of coping strategies.

The Firefighter is adept at dealing with difficult people. They've had lots of experience with challenging personalities. They've been raised by one or been married to one, so they've developed a range of coping skills to deal with those challenges. The trauma and loss the Firefighter experienced pose a challenge for even the most sophisticated copers. However, when a Firefighter takes the time to make sense of their experience and engage in reflection, counseling, and healing, they can develop a depth of character that brings meaning to any engagement they enter.

A Firefighter who has experienced healing produces an uncanny depth of character. They are well-acquainted with so-called character-building experiences and may find that they understand the following passage of Scripture in a way other styles are unable to: "Not only so, but we also glory in our sufferings, because we know that suffering produces perseverance; perseverance, character; and character, hope. And hope does not put us to shame, because God's love has been poured out into our hearts through the Holy Spirit, who has been given to us" (Rom. 5:3–5).

A high-functioning Firefighter eventually transforms into an earned secure Networker. The Firefighter's characteristics of perseverance, hope, and character are hard-won given their climb up the mountain of suffering, but these types of

Firefighters are some of the most compassionate and devoted relationship partners. They have a deep well of hope and an uncommon strength of character. Anyone would be blessed to have them as a partner. However, a Firefighter who isn't willing to slay their dragons and seek healing from past interpersonal wounds will find themselves stuck on a difficult path, circling around the same mountains and struggling to function. They may struggle with addictions and other unhelpful coping mechanisms as a crutch for their precarious, painful journey.

The Journey toward Optimizing the Firefighter's Style

Angela Duckworth, professor of psychology at the University of Pennsylvania, is better known as the author of *GRIT: The Power of Passion and Perseverance*. She argues that if we practice doing hard things regularly, we'll be able to work harder and exert more effort when needed. The moral of the story is doing hard things is good for us; our future selves will thank us because we'll have the stamina to persevere when we're presented with future challenges.

The journey to a high-functioning relationship style is one of those hard things that will positively affect not only our future selves but our future relationship partners as well. A large body of research provides us with many answers about pursuing the path toward a more secure relationship style.

Some Firefighters may grow up with loving and responsive caregivers, similar to the secure Networker, only to experience trauma or loss later in life that leads to a shift in their relationship style. Let's look at an example.

Dr. Viktor Frankl survived life in Nazi concentration camps. His experience in Auschwitz required him to face trauma and loss on a regular basis. He describes life in the camp in his book *Man's Search for Meaning*. All prisoners were assigned a number that was tattooed to their bodies or sewn onto their clothing.

Anytime a guard wanted to charge a prisoner with something, they just looked at the prisoner's number; they never asked for their name. Prisoners' identities were reduced to their numbers. They weren't considered human beings.

Exposure to severe trauma can be part of the Firefighter's experience. Their journey toward optimizing their style may involve encountering sensitive and emotionally intelligent mentors on their journey of becoming. Having a safe place to feel seen and known is an important part of the Firefighter's journey toward an optimized relationship style. Having a partner with eyes to see the best in them can be a healing balm.

This long journey requires utilizing skills and practices recommended for all the relationship styles—but with an extra dose of both patience and grace. The Firefighter struggles with both the avoidant characteristic of the Security Guard's style and the anxiety associated with the Investigator's style. I recommend taking a bio-psycho-social-spiritual approach.

If you are a Firefighter, think of your life in these four circles and ask how you can attend to your needs in each area. It's important to continue doing things in each of these areas every day to move toward healing.

- **Biological**: Medication may help strengthen your PFC activity. Dr. Daniel Amen recommends fish oil for nearly every brain type because omega-3 fatty acids are so good for the brain, and their consumption is associated with reduced inflammation. Check with your doctor to find out the best supplements for you.
- **Psychological**: I recommend embracing personal development reading and therapy. Specifically, I recommend the work of James McCullough, emeritus professor of psychology at Virginia Commonwealth University. McCullough developed a technique used in treatment for depression called a situation analysis in which you think

of a difficult situation and develop your desired outcome, then you keep that outcome in mind and evaluate
whether your behavior is moving you toward that outcome. If not, you take a look at what's stopping you. The
key is the outcome must depend on you. Your outcome
cannot be for your partner to be less annoying or more
loving; instead, it could be for you to more directly articulate your request for more loving behavior. The request
depends on you; the outcome or response is up to them.

- **Social**: Secure interpersonal relationships involve moving toward connection. It's important to work to create
healthy relationships, whether with neighbors, a church
community, colleagues, friends, or family. Try to seek out
those you feel safe with and invest in those relationships.
Be careful to distinguish between *comfortable* and *safe*. In
crisis situations, unsafe has become the norm, and you
may have become comfortable being uncomfortable.

- **Spiritual**: Reflect on the thoughts that cross your mind
when you think about God. Thinking of Him as a loving heavenly Father and nurturing that relationship will
serve as a protective buffer and help compensate for
painful experiences with human relationship figures. I
recommend going to FathersLoveLetter.com/text.html
and reading the Father's Love Letter or watching it on
YouTube.[20] Another helpful resource is the classic book
and lovely allegory *Hinds' Feet on High Places* by Hannah Hurnard. Please visit DrAnitaKuhnley.com for other
resources and an alternate version of the Father's Love
Letter for trauma survivors.

KEY TAKEAWAYS

- High-functioning Firefighters are overcomers of adversity, and they come in multiple types: those with difficult or chaotic experiences and those with experiences of unresolved abuse or loss.
- The Firefighter may be chronically stuck in crisis mode and struggling to shift out of it. At times, they struggle to identify structured responses that work for dealing with emotions and interpersonal relationships, making their style very different from the other styles, which are highly structured in their approaches to both relationships and emotions.
- The low-functioning Firefighter may have a hard time developing trust in romantic relationships, may be overwhelmed with emotion, and may perpetually feel stuck. On the anxiety and avoidance continuum they may be further down, experiencing more intensive levels of anxiety and avoidance than high-functioning Firefighters.
- The Firefighter may have difficulty serving as a safe haven and secure base and may require their partner to have a rich network of support to have a successful relationship.

A CONCEPT TO CONTEMPLATE

Take time to journal and reflect about your relationship history. Go ahead; be brave. Are there any unresolved struggles, perhaps past hurts or fires, that are still holding you back? What kind of impact are they having? What feelings come up as you journal? God invites us to intimacy, which can mean sharing our lament and pain with Him and receiving His comfort. I invite you to work through some of this in your journal.

> *Whoever dwells in the shelter of the Most High*
> *will rest in the shadow of the Almighty.*
> *I will say of the LORD, "He is my refuge and my fortress,*
> *my God, in whom I trust."*
>
> *Psalms 91:1–2*

5

The Investigator

When my youngest brother, Paul, was about five years old, he started coming to ask me to read him a book. And then another book. And another. I read to him every night before bed, and I tried to always say yes when he asked me during the daytime as well. After all, I loved him, I liked books, and he usually said, "Please." Occasionally, I was tired or in a hurry and would try to sneakily skip a few pages, but Paul was an astute observer, and he would call me on it. "Azita! Wait, you skipped this page!" he would protest, using his affectionate nickname for me.

So I would go back and reread them. But truthfully, I did not mind a bit.

Paul was fortunate he was so cute. He had kissable cheeks, and my mom and I both gave him lots of kisses. Once, after some reading time, I gave him some kisses and he started to rub his hand over the spot. "Paul!" I said, now the observant one, "are you wiping off my kisses?"

"Oh no!" he said. "I am not wiping them off, I am rubbing them in!"

The Investigator often needs reassurance that their love is not being wiped away like the kisses on Paul's cheeks. We all deal with inconsistencies from time to time in our relationships with our partners or others, but inconsistency was the Investigator's pervasive experience during childhood, and without intervention, it becomes their experience with their partner as well. The problem is the Investigator is often reluctant to ask for reassurance since they are used to setting aside their needs due to inconsistent responses from caregivers. They often assume they are correct about the other person's unloving behavior and thus operate under assumptions that drive a wedge between them. Worse yet, they are often drawn to the Security Guard, who is less likely to be in tune with their own emotions or responses and much less in tune with the emotions of their Investigator partner. Let's take a closer look.

A Look at Investigators: Rachel

Have you ever gotten all you ever wanted and then realized it was all you never needed?

Rachel did. But in just a few short years, her hopes and her heart would be shattered into shards like broken glass.

Rachel and Peter were both at the ice rink one day. She was skating for relaxation, and he was the most advanced amateur competitive figure skater around. He was tall, dark, and handsome and had a smooth British accent. Rachel was surprised when Peter handed her his business card and invited her on a lunch date. She readily agreed and they met up at the rink café. The two were opposites in many ways: Rachel was open and chatty, while Peter tended to be buttoned-up, defensive, and guarded, at least in the beginning.

However, Peter told Rachel many interesting things about the world of figure skating since Rachel was a newbie. She was enthralled as much with the world of figure skating as she was with Peter, who constantly occupied her thoughts. Rachel told her friends all about him—more than they ever wanted to know—and she couldn't wait until the next date. Peter seemed eager to see her as well. The two went on a flurry of dates and began seeing each other several times a week.

Then, seemingly for no reason, Peter started to pull away. They only saw each other on Saturday nights and some weeks not at all. Rachel was smitten, but no matter how much time and effort she put into the relationship, it didn't seem to matter— Peter was becoming more aloof and disinterested. Yet he didn't break up with her, and Rachel found this puzzling. Before she realized what was happening, Rachel had withdrawn from most of her other friendships because she was so consumed with Peter. She continued to show up for figure skating, but her hope and her general optimistic, positive disposition started to fade as her hopes of romance with Peter fluctuated between somewhat hopeful and devastated on the regular.

Peter had become the center of her life. She waited for his phone calls and hung on his every word, but the harder she tried to be witty and lovable, the more distant Peter became. Rachel was good at setting goals, going after them, and meeting them. She thought if she could just become the figure skater of Peter's dreams and pursue him the right way, he would eventually come around. Rachel thought she could become good enough if she just worked a little harder.

She didn't realize Peter kept pushing her away, not because of something in her but because of something in him. All her striving didn't help the situation. She didn't know how badly she needed a QTIP.

Three years later, Rachel and Peter were still dating and not much had changed for Peter. Rachel, on the other hand, had lost friends, lost her joy, and lost some of her health and fitness. She still loved Peter and remained devoted to him, but she was tired of not being his priority, so she gave him an ultimatum:

"Either we break up and move on with our lives or we decide to take our relationship to the next level and get married."

She wasn't sure she really wanted the answer since Peter had been so uncommunicative, but she knew something had to give. She prayed and decided to give it one week. If he didn't propose by the end of the week, she would walk away. She prayed God would give her the strength to do so.

The week passed slowly, but finally Sunday night came. Peter seemed frozen with indecision as they sat on his couch discussing their relationship. When the clock struck midnight, Rachel, eyes streaming with tears, stood up to leave Peter's house and his life forever. Suddenly, he grabbed her arms and said, "Wait!"

Rachel looked up, sniffling, too shocked to respond.

"I just, I, uh . . . I have a hard time accepting good things into my life," he said, "and I think God is telling me you are a gift from Him. I think He wants me to receive the gift. So, will you marry me?"

Rachel was so awestruck she could barely speak. She disregarded her own discomfort and said a quiet yes.

After several years of marriage, recurring nightmares, and depression, Rachel parted ways with Peter, and they divorced. When Rachel asked her friend what he thought had gone wrong in her relationship with Peter, he said, "Well, I don't think the divorce was the mistake. I think ever marrying him in the first place was the mistake."

Years later in our counseling office, Rachel shook her head as she reflected on what she called her "love drunkenness." As she looked back on that conversation with her friend and most aspects of her relationship with Peter, Rachel saw things she wished she hadn't ignored, but in her heart of hearts, she felt so in love with Peter that she simply overlooked the red flags and focused on all that she admired about him.

Like Rachel, the Investigator often looks for what they want to see in a relationship. They use what we call *researcher's bias* to search out data to support their beliefs—one of which is that the self isn't worthy of love. Unfortunately, sometimes a Security Guard (like Peter) and an Investigator (like Rachel) get together, and it creates the perfect storm. The Security Guard's relationship blueprint says the self is worthy of love but others aren't able to demonstrate love. And the Investigator's relationship blueprint says just the opposite: the self isn't worthy of love but others are able to love. Together, they tend to reinforce the lies that have kept them each fenced in.

The Investigator's Origin Story

Boring isn't a word often used to describe the Investigator (*dramatic* is more likely). Those with the Investigator style often grew up with consistently inconsistent messages from their primary relationship figures, so it was difficult to know when they would experience love and comfort versus when they'd be met with cold indifference or hot rage. To get their needs met, the Investigator often had to up the ante. They may have had to become loud and dramatic to get the attention, love, and care they needed. As adults, they usually wait until their needs are truly urgent before asking for help, care, or love. Thus, they may come across as over-the-top. Others may discount their needs due to their flair for the dramatic, leaving them reenacting patterns from days of old and continuously upping the ante to get attention and have their needs met.

During the darkness of their childhood, the Investigator likely dealt with a combination of mixed messages. Sometimes the messages were loving, and other times they were unloving, rejecting, role-reversing, or neglecting. The only consistency they likely experienced with their primary relationship figures was the vagaries of the capricious caregivers. Thus, change became their constant, and being able to adjust to the changing tides was a requirement for survival. This inconsistency left the Investigator puzzled about the patterns of their caregivers.

To cope with their situation, the Investigator was forced to develop a strategy of investigation and analysis to determine what was coming, also known as preoccupation. The Investigator had to search for any clue that might indicate what to expect. They learned to pay special attention to vocal tone, facial expressions, and other indicators to understand their caregivers' state of mind.

The primary relationship figure of some Investigators reversed roles with them, expecting the child to take care of *their* needs. In these cases, the child learned to set their own needs aside and attend to the adult. Investigators may be used to striving to be who their loved ones want them to be in order to feel loved. They may not have stopped to think about what they really want, feel, think or need. If you ask an Investigator how they like their eggs cooked, they may not be able to tell you; they may not know. From a young age, Investigators mastered the way of the chameleon—altering their colors to suit their changing environmental demands.

The darkness of their childhood cloaked their heart in doubt about their worthiness. They may have felt they had to betray themselves and their own needs to care for their caregiver. As an adult, even in a loving relationship with promises of partnership and presence, the Investigator finds their doubts still linger.

The Investigator's Relationship Blueprint

What impact did consistently inconsistent early relationship experiences have on the Investigator? Well, they set the stage for them to conclude they weren't worthy of love. Or that they could only experience miraculous moments of worthiness by pleasing their caregivers.

Let's take a look at how the Investigator answers the two questions that inform their relationship blueprint.

Am I worthy of love? The Investigator always answers no: "Others *can* meet my needs, but I can't expect them to love me because of my flaws."

Like every lie, there's often a bit of truth woven in. The truth is that this has been the Investigator's interpersonal experience. They believe that when they perform well or are especially adept at taking care of their relationship partner's emotional needs, they will be rewarded with some semblance of love. Perhaps their loved one struggles with a psychological disorder, is sick, overworked, or has deficits beyond their control that limit their capacity for love. In our example, Peter had been struggling with chronic depression and was unable to be fully present and loving toward Rachel. His unloving behavior did not make Rachel any less worthy of love. Rachel was still worthy of love and respect as a person created in the image of God, whether or not her relationship figures were pleased with her behavior. However, even if Rachel knew this cognitively, feeling it emotionally and feeling worthy of love were a different ball game. The greater the resolution of this cognitive dissonance, the less anxiety the Investigator feels and the more high-functioning they are.

The other important question is *Can others be counted on to love me?* The answer here is almost a conclusive yes, but there is a lingering "but," or a loud "yes, but" depending on where the Investigator is on the continuum of relationship anxiety. Unfortunately, due to consistent inconsistency, the Investigator often responds with something like this: "If I work hard enough, I can make them love me." It is important to note that this is a coping mechanism that keeps the Investigator from feeling helpless. If the Investigator blames themselves, then they can do something about it and can try to work harder to earn love. The problem is that belief is not always based on reality.

The falsehoods in these relational blueprints keep the Investigator trapped in a cycle of endlessly pursuing the elusive love that they desire mixed with the belief that they will never be good enough to be loved. They also keep their true self hidden under a cloak of not-good-enough thoughts, feelings, and behaviors. They're stuck in a people-pleasing mode that helps them feel safe while also preventing them from getting to know themselves.

So they stay trapped in a perpetual search. They're looking for something that's always been just beyond their reach—a forever home for their heart that can only be found on the other side of eternity. Their behaviors and the inconsistent responses they receive deceive them, fueling the belief that if they're good enough, someone will love them. They often betray themselves and become whatever their relationship partner desires.

Yet they're always plagued with doubt about the veracity of that love. The Investigator's mind is preoccupied with a flower game, pulling off each petal and pondering, "They love me, they love me not, they love me, they love me not . . . Which is it today?" They are preoccupied, in search of an affirmative answer to the question, *Am I worthy of love?* They're deceived by the false hope that if they work hard enough, just maybe someday they'll find a convincing, "Yes, a thousand times, yes."

Emotions and the Investigator

The Investigator has a clear trajectory in relationships. They tend to move circuitously toward connection, but there's a problem that prevents them from making authentic connection. They anxiously grip their magnifying glass, eagerly seeking to analyze the signals their partners send: "Which partner will I get today, the distant, angry, or rejecting partner? Or will it be the loving, kind, and available partner?" The Investigator has high levels of relationship anxiety, and this strong current of anxiety can flood them at times, dysregulating their emotions.

Unfortunately, their own preoccupation and analysis cause them to get tangled up in a self-fulfilling prophecy—they tend to find what they look for.

Some years ago, I was involved in a two-car accident, and the experience left me shaken—and it totaled my car. So I began researching cars with high scores for safety and came across the Subaru's outstanding record. I had never really noticed Subarus, but now I saw them everywhere. I was finding what I was looking for. Maybe you have had a similar experience.

Likewise, when an Investigator is worried or concerned about their relationship partner's tendencies, they become keenly aware when their loved one checks out another attractive partner or checks their phone rather than listening at dinner. These small slights confirm their suspicions. The only thing the Investigator wants their loved one to check out is them. (If their partner is a Security Guard, this is an unlikely outcome.)

When the Investigator sees their partner's hints of half-hearted love, they point out things like "You didn't call to say you were running late. You must not value my time." The partner feels defensive and may launch a countercriticism—and thus conflict begins, leading to entanglement. The Investigator may find themselves entangled with emotions or overwhelmed by them. Let's look at how this manifests:

- The Investigator struggles with higher levels of anxiety. They may have an overactive sympathetic nervous system—the part of the nervous system that's activated in dangerous situations—that's overaroused.
- The Investigator may be uncomfortable sharing their emotions. They're used to hiding or stuffing those emotions and setting them aside. When emotions do reach the point that they overflow from their restricted

containment, they can be very big, with needs and more vulnerable feelings wrapped in anger and resentment, making them more difficult for their partners to swallow. Investigators are prone to tension-reduction behaviors such as consuming alcohol or smoking marijuana or other addictive behaviors.

- The Investigator may have been required to reverse roles with their caregiver as a child. They may have been responsible for their caregiver's feelings and were made to feel guilty about having any needs of their own. Their anxiety triggers them to overexplain, and they may feel more comfortable attending to *their partner's* emotions.

- Asking the Investigator to have an opinion can be a challenge at times, as they may have difficulty expressing their own thoughts and opinions. When asked where they want to go to dinner, they may say, "Wherever. Can you pick?"

- The Investigator tends to be empathic and attentive to their partner's emotions but awkward when they are irritated. Their partner may detect the undercurrent of hostility without knowing why.

- The Investigator makes an incredible actor because they know how to portray an emotion. Acting provides an outlet to express aspects of themselves they've had to hide and suppress for years.

- Painful emotions such as anger may emerge as passive-aggressive or hostile-dominant in interpersonal relationships. The Investigator may not be comfortable expressing those emotions directly and vulnerably, so they'll have emotional eruptions at inopportune times. These may look like dysregulated outbursts of anger and overwhelming feelings of sadness.

- There is often a hidden plea for connection or a softer suggestion or request underlying the irritable exasperation that the Investigator's partner may miss because it sounds sour. For example, if the Investigator makes a barbed comment such as "We never spend any time together! Why are you always busy?" their partner may hear criticism. Because of the defensive and somewhat hostile wrapper the comment is delivered in, the Investigator's partner may interpret the words as "you are inept and are a disappointment" rather than the underlying request to spend more time together.

Understanding the Investigator

If you have the Investigator's relationship style, you'll probably understand the concern of loving your partner more than they love you. If you're dating a Security Guard, that concern is probably confirmed. The Investigator may not be self-aware. As the chameleon changes colors to find safety in their environment, so the Investigator changes colors to find love. Early in their journey of becoming, the Investigator is prone to mood disorders and higher levels of anxiety or depression but is also likely to be in counseling and pursuing the path toward a higher-functioning relationship style.[1]

Growing up in an inconsistent environment, their experiences may have convinced them that they didn't know whether their important relationship figures would abandon them. As a child, when their caregivers returned after leaving them in the nursery with a stranger for a brief time, the Investigator may have expressed anger that they were left alone, and that anger manifested in the child resisting the mother's embrace or bodily contact.[2] Likewise, the Strange Situation also revealed that Networkers tended to be quickly soothed and showed more positive emotion and delight when their caregiver returned, while Investigators displayed more anger and took longer to calm down.[3]

As the Investigator grows older and their primary relationship figures become spouses, partners, or family members, they maintain the same relatively stable relationship patterns unless they take the time to revise and rewrite their relationship blueprint. They may continue to worry that their important relationship figures will abandon them physically and emotionally. It's important to think back to the Circle of Security in chapter 2 and discuss it with a counselor.

God as Our Safe Haven

Thankfully, there's One who will never leave us or forsake us. Having a relationship with God can be a source of healing and support for Investigators who have mild levels of anxiety. However, Dr. Gary Sibcy has researched *doubt* and found that with some of the anxious clients he works with, this may not be the case.[4] If an Investigator has had a more severe background and has high levels of relationship-related anxiety, they may project that anxiety and doubt onto God. If their anxiety levels are low, then a relationship with God may help compensate for a sense of unloving experiences during childhood.

Just as relationally the Investigator fears they're on a journey to find love that has no destination and no end, they fear their love and vulnerable emotions and desires will never find a home in a partner who eludes them. They may find comfort in knowing that human relationships are limited and cannot offer 100 percent fulfillment, but the fullness of joy is something they may find through worship and intimacy with God. This may help with expectation setting and radical acceptance.

Developing a Testimony

One key marker some relationship researchers use to determine the degree to which a person's style is secure and high-functioning is to see if they can tell their relationship story in a clear and coherent way. This story has been called different names: autobiographical narrative, relationship narrative, relationship story, or glory story. To some, it's known as a testimony. Some attachment researchers call it a coherent narrative. Except for the prototypical Networker, many people have to overcome a test of sorts and make sense of painful experiences in order to develop their testimony. Most people do not come by a coherent testimony without paying a price. No one can share their testimony without first taking their test, so to speak.

Developing this testimony and overcoming and calming the current of anxiety can be especially challenging for the Investigator. Semantics scholar Mariëlle Beijersbergen and her colleagues found certain patterns were central to some relationship styles.[5] Linguistic philosopher Paul Grice developed four requirements a conversationalist needs to ensure a conversation is collaborative. These include the ability to

1. tell the truth and provide evidence to support your assertions,
2. be concise while also being complete,
3. be relevant and on topic, and
4. speak with clarity and order.

The Networker follows all of these rules well. However, other styles follow certain patterns that violate these rules in predictable ways. The Investigator finds it difficult to be both concise and complete. Their stories are longer, so it's hard to find the right words to describe their experience when their mind is caught up with fear or anger related to their important relationships. They have also experienced inconsistencies, which makes it more tempting to oscillate back and forth when trying to make sense of the nonsense. This makes it more difficult to dialogue cooperatively and tell their interpersonal story.

Investigators may find themselves at a loss for words or stuck throughout the story, using passive speech like, "You know, that kind of a thing," or "This, that, and the other."[6] Relationship science researchers describe the Investigator's storytelling tendencies in this way: "They tell long stories, drift away from the main topic of the question, and use angry or passive speech."[7]

Like math tests, interpersonal tests (or challenges) can evoke test anxiety—especially for the Investigator. Test anxiety may interfere with the Investigator's ability to be fully present to collaboratively communicate about their testimony. The good news in this case is that the reward for test anxiety is not failure. Life offers second chances. The Investigator's reward for their anxiety and relational failures is not eternal failure but rather the opportunity to retake the same relational tests repeatedly until they pass and graduate to elevated security. We have many words for these challenging times. We may call it the dark night of the soul, wandering in the wilderness, a winter season, or an uphill journey. The Investigator is familiar with these relational word pictures.

They may feel like they are wandering in the wilderness or struggling to listen to the still, small voice inside that is being drowned out by noisy anxieties and fears. The good news is, despite the Investigator's comfort with being uncomfortable, they are not destined to stay stuck, circling the same relational mountains for life. Some of the characters in the Bible who were greatly used by God experienced significant relational tests. Consider Joseph, who was betrayed by his brothers and thrown into a pit; Esther, who stood between her husband and the slaughtering of her family of origin; or even Jesus, who was betrayed by a close friend and on the cross shouted out, "My God, my God, why have you forsaken me?" (Matt. 27:46).

The Investigator, too, may feel forsaken by God. They may pray what theologian Richard J. Foster calls "The Prayer of the Forsaken," wondering where God is and where consistent loving presence is in their moment of distress.[8] Yet He is there with them in the cry. The Investigator can, through their journey with the Lord and other tools, such as counseling, journaling, bibliotherapy, and Bible study, seek to revise their narrative and make sense of this journey. Therapists are often adept at helping Investigators ask the existential questions and find meaning in their suffering, which is a reminder that God can use all of our experiences, even the painful ones, since they are all

God can use all of our experiences, even the painful ones.

part of the beautiful love story the Lover of our souls and the Author and Finisher of our faith is writing for our lives.

Loving the Investigator

How do you recognize if you're in a relationship with an Investigator?

- It's hard to get a straight answer from them. With the Investigator, there is always another perspective to consider due to the inconsistencies they experienced in their past.
- It's difficult to end phone conversations and enforce boundaries. The end of a call or date may feel like abandonment and activates the Investigator's relationship system, triggering anxiety.
- It seems like they reside in Shouldville, believing you "should" act or behave in a particular way or intuitively know and respond to their needs.
- You get mixed signals, sometimes sensing you have upset your partner but don't know why. When you ask what's wrong, you get a very unbelievable "Nothing, I am FINE!" in response.

The Investigator has a flair for drama and may get tangled up when they're trying to express feelings or share stories from their relationship history. However, there are a few things you can do to help the Investigator feel loved and more secure.

Ask with Patience

Feelings are natural, and they provide us with important information. The Investigator may have been made to feel guilty for having personal feelings, needs, or desires, or they may have grown up with messages socializing them against expressing feelings, like, "Turn that frown upside down," "Children are to be seen and not heard," or "Don't complain or I'll give you something to complain about." These factors make it challenging for the Investigator to express their feelings and needs.

You can help the Investigator by asking them what they need, especially when they're under stress. Patience is a needed ingredient since they may not have been allowed to express feelings in the past. If you ask, "What do you need?" or "What can I do to help?" they may get defensive and not have an answer. Remember, the Investigator may have stuffed their upset feelings about something for so long that they now have built-up resentment, and their comment or request may come in such a stiff package of bitterness and resentment that it is tough to open it up and find the Investigator's hidden hope for connection and love.

You can make an Investigator feel more comfortable opening up by providing a suggestion. Rather than asking "How can I help?" try something more specific, like, "Can I give you a massage after your call with your mom? I know that's stressful for you." Or "Would you like me to come with you to your doctor's appointment?"

Develop Reframing Skills

The Investigator often forgets their QTIPs. This is unfortunate since they usually need a whole box of them! To prepare for this, it helps to grow in the grace of reframing. Reframing is clinical phraseology for what happens when we describe a situation differently to gain a new perspective. The story about my brother Paul rubbing in my kisses is one of my favorite examples of reframing.

Sprinkle Loving Words like Confetti

Look for opportunities to show and express love to the Investigator. They may benefit from all five love languages, and reassurances of your love and consistency with words and actions will also help to build trust. Genuine generous effusive language may be an effective healing balm (especially if words of affirmation are their love language). Try pairing loving words such as "I love you and am thankful for you" with loving actions such as opening their car door or helping them with a chore. This will help them resolve the cognitive dissonance between their seeking to move toward the secure belief that they are worthy of love and the lingering emotional sense that they are unworthy of love that even high-functioning Investigators struggle to shake. As trust builds, it becomes easier for the Investigator to turn toward their partner with less reactivity and entanglement.[9]

If direct and kind communication of feelings and needs is your strong suit, you can model this for your Investigator. Letting them know you are interested in their feelings and helping them give themselves permission to express their wants and needs can be helpful.

Be Consistent

The Investigator has long craved consistency, yet they have often grown comfortably uncomfortable with its elusiveness. You can unlock your Investigator's sense of safety with reassurance (when needed) and a comfortable routine. Find a consistent routine for your relationship by adding structure to your relationship. Consistency and congruence help the Investigator be their most secure self with you. Consider these ideas:

- Snuggle-up Sundays—take a nap together or snuggle up with a good book and read together.
- Sabbath Sunday—go to church and have a special dinner at home, then pray over the next week. (This may work well with a Security Guard, as research shows that God-attachment interventions, such as contemplative prayer and God images, decrease avoidance.)
- Massage Mondays—offer your Investigator a massage before bed with no expectation of more, though you may be pleasantly surprised. The oxytocin and the consistency are both helpful.
- Taco Tuesday—set a regular date night with your Investigator at home or out on the town.
- Choose terms of endearment they are comfortable with and use them.
- Let them know how you feel and express those feelings as often as possible.

Be Intentional

By sharing your intentions with your Investigator, you'll help them put away their magnifying glass. For example, if you say, "I can't eat dinner after six. If you aren't down and ready by then, you can heat up your food and eat alone," the Investigator will be left holding a giant clue that looks and smells like evidence you don't love them. They'll likely put on their boxing gloves or running shoes and go into fight-or-flight mode.

On the other hand, if you say, "Honey, I'd like to talk with you about something. If we could work on it together it would help me feel better. I'm starving by six, but I really want to eat dinner with you. Would you be willing to eat earlier? And if not, would it be OK if I started dinner without you? I think it is best for both of us if I do not get too hangry." Remember to start softly and maybe end with a wink or a smile.

The Secret to Loving the Investigator

Investigators need to be loved for who they are rather than what they do. They've had to work hard to earn love either through role reversal, swallowing their own needs, or using their chameleon-like creativity. They are inclined to look for signs that you don't love or care for them. Try to reassure your Investigator that you love them not because of their appearance or performance but because of their personality, kindness, intellectual camaraderie, or other personal traits or ways of being. The secret to loving the Investigator is revealed by the fox in the children's story *The Little Prince*: "One sees clearly only with the heart. Anything essential is invisible to the eyes."[10] Look at the Investigator with eyes to see their resourceful spirit that has helped them overcome much adversity, their anxiety as a tool to help them avoid pain and peril, and their vulnerable feelings often wrapped up in harsh words and irritability.

When you have a critique for your Investigator or a request for change, remind them that your relationship is secure. Consider the difference between these two statements:

Option 1: "Don't spend any money. We cannot afford it right now."

Option 2: "Sweetheart, I love you very much, and I want to make sure we have enough to take care of all of our bills. Will you help me by limiting spending until after Christmas?"

Investigators often find themselves in relationships with Security Guards—there seems to be a magnetic pull between these two styles. Some say they are drawn to each other for all the wrong reasons. Why? Their relationship blueprints complement each other in a maladaptive way. For example, the

Investigator believes they aren't worthy of love but that other people are able to show love, so they believe their partner would be inclined to pursue them and treat them better if they were more lovable.

Meanwhile, the Security Guard feels uncomfortable with the Investigator's closeness and believes they don't respect the Security Guard's belief that they are worthy of love but that others may not be competent to show them love. In some ways, they both experience *confirmation bias*: they each find evidence to confirm their own biases. This keeps them stuck in a dysfunctional interpersonal loop.

If you (the Security Guard) and your partner (the Investigator) share a Christian faith, it may be helpful to nudge your partner toward the truth that they aren't an orphan. They've been adopted as a child of God. It's important to ask the questions, Am I living as a child of God or as an orphan? Am I striving and scratching to earn the worthiness to be loved? Or am I resting in the love of my heavenly Father who longs to lavish His love upon me simply because I am His? (1 John 3:1). It is worth revisiting these questions each time we notice our tendency to seek to earn love.

God announces His love for us through His words. He whispers it through the subtle breeze on a hot day and the crimson slice of sunshine ducking behind the clouds, casting its rays across the sky and reflecting on the water. Do you have ears to hear and eyes to see what the Creator is communicating to you? Or are your ears turned toward the world's roaring and rumbling rant that you aren't enough, that you aren't needed, wanted, or loved? Remember, we tend to hear what we're listening for, and what we attend to and think about is magnified by our meditation.

A key feature of the Investigator's style is anxiety about abandonment and inconsistencies that manifest in relationships. I work with a team of colleagues and graduate students and through our research on treatments to help people become more secure, we've found that participating in mindful self-compassion exercises results in a slight decrease in anxiety regarding relationship with God and a significant decrease in avoidance related to relationship to God.[11] In these exercises, participants practice showing kindness to themselves, acknowledging moments of suffering, and recognizing they're part of common humanity.

Other recent studies indicate that the more we show self-kindness, the less anxious we are about our relationship.[12] This can help Investigators experience the loving-kindness they missed out on growing up. Thus, it may be helpful to show extra levels of compassion toward your Investigator partner and encourage them to be compassionate toward themselves.

Benefits of the Investigator's Style

If you're an Investigator, you developed this style out of repeated relational rebuffs, slights, and inconsistencies, intermingled with some loving behaviors and experiences, that spanned many years. This style helped you navigate the sometimes scary and very uncertain terrain of an uncertain home life—and it likely helped you develop skills that elevate your emotional intelligence and empathy.

The Investigator has many strengths, including the following:

- The Investigator is attuned to the emotions of others and is often sensitive to their partner's feelings.
- The Investigator feels very deeply; they are likely the last to be accused of being cold or lukewarm.
- The Investigator, despite past experiences, tends to value relationships and longs to be loved.

- The Investigator often applies psychology, human development, and personal knowledge to understand their relationship dynamics.
- The Investigator is generous with words and is often a good conversationalist.
- The Investigator's relationship blueprint makes it a bit easier for them to take responsibility for their part in relationship struggles, which is promising for change.
- The high-functioning Investigator develops strong self-awareness and metacognitive monitoring. They are aware of their anxieties and are learning to voice them in a way that is not overwhelming. In a healthy relationship, they can learn to accept reassurance.

These characteristics are an asset and can help the Investigator overcome issues stemming from an unreliable caregiver. The Investigator's experiences forced them to develop a unique skill set that may serve them well on the journey to earning relationship security.

The Journey toward Optimizing the Investigator's Style

The dryness of doubt in the Investigator's throat leaves them thirsting for the reassurance of love and connection, which is delightfully incongruent with their past journey. This thirst may motivate them to pursue the journey to healing and earned security. They may be willing to face the uncomfortable experiences required for a course correction.

It's important for the Investigator to remember a specific distinction: just because their anxious thoughts are *loud*, that does not make them *true*. The Investigator does well to turn down the volume on these lies, facing the challenge of quelling the noise until it's quiet enough to hear the whisper of an unlikely truth. One of the Investigator's greatest challenges to becoming more secure is coming to terms with the dissonance between their experiential sense of being unworthy of love and their cognitive knowledge of their worthiness of love. The Investigator is worthy of love, and life can offer second chances for them to experience those loving relationships if they stay open to unlikely opportunities. God still has a plan for the Investigator. However, if the Investigator does not do the work to come to terms with this truth, there is little others can do to convince them of their lovability.

> *The Investigator is worthy of love, and life can offer second chances for them to experience those loving relationships.*

One benefit of the Investigator reducing their relationship anxiety is an increase in the stability of their self-esteem.[13] The Investigator's journey toward security may be a long and circuitous route. However, when the Investigator is ready to face the darkness of their painful romantic experiences or their difficult childhood experiences and relational blueprints in light of how they're darkening present relationships, there's hope. They can experience change.

Anxiety and the Investigator

An Investigator's tendency toward anxiety about their partner's intentions can alienate partners who don't have their QTIPs. It's important for the Investigator to recognize their anxiety and tendency to fret about their partner's intentions. It may be helpful to journal and get feelings out on paper before uttering the often-dreaded words to their partner: "We need to talk." Investigators may struggle to grasp control of a situation or a person.

My colleague, who we will call Jane, once mentioned that she wanted to change her husband. She didn't want him to be into sports, so she tried to influence him away from them. One day she saw him in the living room, listening to a baseball game on the radio, watching a football game, and polishing his snowboard. At that point, she had an epiphany. Jane realized what she was doing wasn't working. She decided to relinquish control to God and leave her husband in His hands. Now she is able to look back at her efforts with a smile. May each Investigator have this experiential epiphany early in their journey toward security.

Investigators who draw upon their relationship with God may find that He was there in the shadows all along. Although they couldn't physically see Him in their moment of despair, His presence and love were constants.

They may find doubt popping into their relationship with God as well. Their relationship history makes it easy for them to take this leap of doubt into their relationship with God. However, He's strong enough to handle that. Like the psalmist, the Investigator can take solace in pouring out their heart to their heavenly Father. A good example is Psalm 42, where the psalmist says he thirsts for God like a deer thirsts for streams of water. The psalmist acknowledges his soul is downcast, but then encourages himself to put his trust in the Lord:

> *Why, my soul, are you downcast?*
> *Why so disturbed within me?*
> *Put your hope in God,*
> *for I will yet praise him,*
> *my Savior and my God.* (Ps. 42:5)

Though the Investigator's doubt makes it challenging for them to trust God's promises, taking their doubt to Him and sitting with their questions and His answers can bring comfort and peace. When Investigators can be kind and compassionate to themselves about their struggles (including doubts), their anxiety decreases. Becoming anxious about being anxious does no good and can be an even harder monster to manage than anxiety itself.

The Toxic Coping Skill

Some Investigators may struggle with a corrosive and cruel tendency that interferes with their relationships—and it's more prominent in their relationship story than that of the other styles. It's the tendency to use the toxic practice of blaming. The Investigator doesn't discriminate when it comes to blame; they may blame themselves or they may blame others.

Dr. David Burns, a psychiatrist and author of one of the most influential books on fighting depression, *Feeling Good Together*, developed an intervention that's been helpful for dealing with blame. Burns discusses the idea of doing a Blame Cost-Benefit Analysis. The result of this analysis reveals whether Burns suggests he as a therapist can help. Grab a blank sheet of paper. On the left, write all the benefits of blame, such as "You can be angry and resentful—anger is empowering." On the right side of the page, list all the costs of blame, such as "You'll feel frustrated and resentful because nothing will change."[14] After you make a list as long as you can in both columns, assign a point value to each column. Some costs may pose a greater expense than others (it's subjective). If the benefits of blame (i.e., avoiding taking responsibility) outweigh the costs (i.e., feeling stuck and resentful), Burns's theory reveals that nothing can help this relationship if one of the romantic partners chooses to hang on to blame. More specifically, Burns says,

> *Blame is too powerful an adversary for me. It's the atom bomb of intimacy. It destroys everything that gets in its way. I'm not aware of any techniques that are powerful enough to help people who blame others for the problems in their relationships. . . . You might do better to focus on a different relationship with someone who's more important to you.*[15]

If the costs and benefits of blame on your sheet are equivalent, Burns also indicates he cannot help. He validates the idea that though it does seem perfectly acceptable to ask others to take responsibility for their part of the problem, it does not work.

It is very painful to take responsibility for our problems. A powerful motivator in life is the avoidance of pain. According to Burns, if you want better relationships, help is possible only if you are willing to focus *exclusively* on your own role. Further, his research has revealed that one of the most important predictors of marital bliss is whether or not a person blames their partner for their problems (associated with problems and unhappiness), or whether they take full responsibility for their role in the relationship and seek to contribute to their partner's happiness (associated with more fulfilling relationships).[16] Blame is so bad for relationships that Burns describes it this way: "Blame is arguably the most toxic and addictive mindset of all. It competes fiercely with our desires for love."[17] Giving up blame—both blaming the self and others—may be one of the most important challenges for the Investigator in the journey of becoming. It involves exchanging what you want right *now* for what you want *most*.

Dr. John Bowlby also wrote about this tendency to blame.[18] He indicated that children who grew up with caregivers who created a stable atmosphere tended to express concern and distress two or three times as much as they expressed anger or blame. Children who were raised in families that had the dynamics that Firefighters, Investigators, and Security Guards experienced tended to express at least as many fault-finding and angry expressions as they did expressions of distress and concern. Interestingly, many years later, Dr. John Gottman and his colleagues have found that there is a difference in this ratio: stable, happy couples tend to have positive interactions five times more frequently than negative interactions.[19] So, it may be helpful for the Investigator to slip on their rose-tinted sunglasses and remember to look for the positive and express it in their relationships.

As you can imagine, a blaming tone isn't the key to the most loving, warm, and intimate relationship. If your partner has pointed a finger at you, chances are, the other four are pointed back at themselves. If they struggle with blame and a more anxious relationship style, I suggest an intervention practice that is linked to reducing that anxiety: self-compassion meditations. One goal on the journey to earning security is seeking to eliminate self-blame from the narrative.

Sometimes that self-blame spills out to others. It's important for the Investigator to eliminate blame of others and self. Blame is associated with preoccupying anger and can interfere with the Investigator's ability to be fully present. It can take a long time to change some of these thought patterns.

A signpost on the journey toward reducing relationship anxiety can be going to see a therapist. It's important for the Investigator to find a psychologist or counselor they can build a trusting, therapeutic alliance with. The Investigator needs a safe therapist who has eyes to see them and ears to hear past their pain and blame.

In addition, the Investigator may benefit from a relationship coach or from a structured program. If the Investigator is struggling with preoccupation with a relationship, it may be helpful to do some work that helps redirect that energy. My friends and colleagues Ellen Fein and Sherry Schneider wrote books entitled *The Rules for Marriage* and *Not Your Mother's Rules* that may help female Investigators who are preoccupied with their relationships to take a step back, remember they're a "creature unlike any other," and discover their own interests and needs.[20]

Investigators use a number of other strategies to decrease the anxiety, fear, and anger associated with painful relationship histories and increase the capacity to be present. For a more comprehensive road map for navigating the journey from the

Investigator's style to an earned secure Networker's style, see chapter 8.

KEY TAKEAWAYS

- The Investigator has a history of consistent inconsistency with their earliest relationship figures.
- The Investigator has keen observational skills and tends to be sensitive to perceived slights.
- The Investigator's relationship blueprint suggests that they aren't worthy of love and that they can't count on others to love them.
- The Investigator is preoccupied with anger or fear regarding their relationship story.
- The Investigator feels anxious or worried that they love their partner more than their partner loves them.
- The Investigator is very attentive and invested in their relationships; they value relationships and turn toward them.

A CONCEPT TO CONTEMPLATE

If you are an Investigator, you may remember a moment in time when you realized—out of the clear blue sky—that your feelings and well-being *did not matter* to your important relationship figures, that it was up to you. Do you remember that moment? How old were you? What did it feel like? If you could go back to that moment now, what would you say to your past self? If you felt shame for having emotions and feelings about things, God has a promise just for you. Consider writing down the following verse in your journal and giving it some thought.

> *Instead of your shame*
>   *you will receive a double portion,*
> *and instead of disgrace*
>   *you will rejoice in your inheritance.*
> *And so you will inherit a double portion in your land,*
>   *and everlasting joy will be yours.*
>
> *Isaiah 61:7*

6

The Security Guard

It was Taco Tuesday at a quaint restaurant in Lynchburg, Virginia, our favorite spot for truly authentic Mexican cuisine and the best tacos in the Hill City! The restaurant was called La Carreta—Spanish for "the road." This particular Tuesday, I had an evening appointment, and I stopped in to pick up some takeout for the group. I ran inside and had an unexpected encounter I would reflect on for some time to come.

I met a charismatic manager whose English was exceptional. His name was Elias. As Elias confirmed my order, I made one last request. "Oh, and would you tell me the name of that white sauce?"

"The Ranchero sauce?" he asked with a smile.

"Oh, is that what it is called?" I had always wondered what this mysterious pool of white goodness really was. "That sauce is delicious! What is in it?" I asked.

Elias leaned in close and lowered his voice to a whisper. "Can you keep a secret?" he asked. Very interested, I nodded and leaned in to make sure I did not miss what he said. As I turned my ear toward him, he whispered, "So can I!"

Just like Elias, the Security Guard may lead you to believe they are going to share the ingredients of their relationship history that helped form the person they are today. When you ask, "How would you describe your childhood relationship with your mom?" they may say, "It was loving." But when you lean in to ask for an example, they might reply with something like, "It was loving because it was caring." The answer is a non-answer or a way of avoiding or dismissing the question. They may give you an answer of sorts, but it does not satisfy all the maxims of collaborative communication. The real answer is never said aloud. The Security Guard may leave you wondering what those relationship history ingredients are. The Security Guard has had to cope with rejection and dismissing caregivers, so they have learned to minimize needing and wanting and tend to dismiss their own needs, feelings, and relational interests, as well as those of the people they are in relationship with. Let's consider Jonah's journey.

A Look at Security Guards: Jonah

As Jonah prepared to visit his mother, who had been diagnosed with late-stage cancer, he and his girlfriend, Sabrina, stood next to his Tesla. Jonah said, "Sabrina, I don't think you've ever really experienced overwhelming pain like this in your life."

She paused for a moment, puzzled by the irony of the accusation. She'd been overwhelmed with heartache and emotional pain trying to figure out how to connect with him—the aloof man she loved. With a smile that belied her anxious heart, Sabrina confessed, "Of course I have experienced pain—I am dating *you!*"

"Touché," Jonah responded with a faint smile. It was the first time his scowl cracked into a smile in a long while. Then he hopped into his Tesla and drove away. Jonah closed Sabrina out and dismissed any effort she made to provide comfort and support.

His behavior was significant. First, he'd pursued Sabrina, then he withdrew. He left her questions unanswered. "Why is Jonah this way?" Sabrina often asked herself. "Is there something wrong with me?"

Our relationship styles find their origins in our early experiences, and Sabrina received a clue at a family lunch she attended with Jonah (a rare occurrence).

It was a cool spring day, and Jonah's family pressured him to attend a lunch with them. Sabrina listened to the family conversation. Jonah's sister said that sometimes she wondered if her baby hated her, because she would cry for long periods of time, constantly disrupting everything. Sabrina cringed as she thought of an innocent infant not likely to cry to manipulate caregivers but rather to get needs met.

Then Jonah's father said, "Don't worry, when your mom worked nights and I was at home with your brother, he would cry his head off. I would go out to the garage to work. The kid would cry in his crib for hours—drove me crazy."

Sabrina looked around, concerned, as she imagined poor baby Jonah all alone, learning that no one was coming for him. Now he was pushing her away as if he were still that poor child.

Jonah's uncle remarked, "Well, that sure explains a lot!" They all chuckled, and Sabrina bit back tears.

In Jonah's first serious, marriage-minded relationship, he had briefly leaned into the discomfort of loving Sabrina, but then leaned away again, keeping her at arm's length. Jonah pushed her away. He shortened phone calls. He was only available to see her once a week and felt overwhelmed when they did spend a long evening together.

When it came to defining their relationship of two years, he said he wanted to keep things casual. There was something nice about having Sabrina around, but he could not shake the feeling of being smothered when she tried to get close, and he always felt ambivalent and a bit unsure about the relationship. There was a part of him that loved Sabrina and felt she was a gift. He did not really want to let her go, but sometimes he just was not sure and wanted some space. He eventually went riding off into the sunset as a single man. He was sorry it did not work out but relieved he could do whatever he wanted.

The Security Guard's Origin Story

Why were relationships so hard for Jonah? It all began long before Sabrina came into the picture. Before he ever had words to verbally reject someone, he was rejected. As a baby, Jonah would sit in his crib, longing for caregivers to scoop him up. His mother, who worked odd hours, followed her parents' advice not to spoil her baby. When she was at work, Jonah's father was left with the baby and would often head out to the garage, following his wife's advice: "Don't you spoil that baby by giving him too much attention." Baby Jonah eventually learned that crying to obtain his needs wouldn't help—no one was coming for him.

In the absence of a consistently available person to meet his emotional needs, Jonah simply turned away. He learned that if he cried too much or pursued attention, he would irritate the important caregivers in his life and risk further alienation. As a result, he turned away from relationships and turned toward tangible objects that he could rely upon—like his teddy bear. He became independent, placing higher value on competence than relationships. He beat the world to the rejection punch.

As a grown-up, Jonah wasn't a bad guy. He had a lot to offer. He was brilliant, athletic, and well-spoken. He could even be charming when he wanted to be. However, his relationship history taught him something important: mistrust. Like most

Security Guards, he learned that interpersonal relationships can be dangerous and marked with rejection. To protect himself, he found it was important to keep a "safe distance."

The whisper of doubt—no one is coming for you—from Jonah's painful childhood experience transformed into a shout in adulthood: "You are on your own. No one cares. They are so unreliable." "You will never get married." "There is no intelligent match for you." These doubts were so loud that Jonah thought they were true, and he built his relational blueprint and interpersonal history upon them.

Let's look at how Jonah's history taught him aspects of the Security Guard's state of mind that guided his interactions with Sabrina:

- The Security Guard believes love is painful. They believe those they love and depend upon will reject them and push them away, so it's best to keep a safe distance.

- The Security Guard minimizes the need for support to protect themselves from rejection. They're likely to become a loner. They prefer their own company over the risk-laden world of interpersonal relationships.

- The Security Guard believes expressing vulnerability will further alienate loved ones, so it's best to suppress needs and feelings. The Security Guard perceives vulnerability as weakness. As a result, they may be disconnected from the world of emotions and interact in a more concrete manner.

- The Security Guard suppresses their needs and emotions so much that they are not in touch with their own feelings or those of their partner.

- The Security Guard may find some comfort and refuge in the constancy of objects, such as collections or toys or activities that numb the gnawing pain of loneliness.

As a function of repeated rejection, the gates around Jonah's heart clanged shut. This put a safe distance between him and his romantic partners' overtures or rejections, but it also closed him off from his own emotions, needs, and hope of true intimacy.

The Security Guard's Relationship Blueprint

The two guiding conclusions our prototypical Security Guard, Jonah, drew from his interpersonal story are, "Others aren't able to show me reliable love, so I'll keep a safe distance" and "I am competent and worthy of love, but I likely won't experience love from others due to the flaws of my relationship partners."

It's important to remember that the Security Guard's relational blueprint was informed by their experiences and also served to get their relationship needs met. Their objective as a child was to maintain a safe closeness to a rejecting caregiver to continue to get basic needs met for survival. Because our relationship blueprints tend to be largely subconscious, Jonah wasn't even aware that as an adult he was in some ways promoting the very rejection he feared.

Meanwhile, the lie that others are incompetent when it comes to love and that no one will ever be there to love him was tenacious. It wrapped itself around Jonah's soul, separating him from any inkling of intimacy. On his journey toward becoming an aware and high-functioning Security Guard, Jonah will need to continuously nudge himself in the uncomfortable direction of the truth.

The Security Guard's faith can be a resource on this journey. Here are some encouraging Scriptures, a few signposts that may point them toward the truth of the love available to them:

Be strong and courageous. Do not be afraid or terrified because of them, for the LORD your God goes with you; he will never leave you nor forsake you. (Deut. 31:6)

Never will I leave you;
never will I forsake you. (Heb. 13:5)

For I am the LORD *your God*
who takes hold of your right hand
and says to you, Do not fear;
I will help you. (Isa. 41:13)

Cast all your anxiety on him because he cares for you.

(1 Pet. 5:7)

Emotions and the Security Guard

In addition to developing a blueprint with respect to relationship expectations, early experiences also help us develop a blueprint that guides our responses to emotions. The Security Guard is often not in tune with their emotions. Research reveals that during childhood, the Security Guard often felt an undercurrent of anger toward their caregiver for not being available and for rejecting their attempts at seeking closeness. They had to stifle their anger to get their needs met and to ensure they lived to face another day.

If you feel disconnected from your emotions, uncomfortable with emotional displays, have a desire to avoid drama like the plague, and have been accused of being aloof, emotionally unavailable, or withdrawn, you may be a Security Guard.

Brain Science and the Security Guard

The Security Guard is well-acquainted with the practice of trying to downplay feelings of needing another person's support, missing someone, or wanting company. These feelings can be uncomfortable. They may also find that they struggle to identify what they want in a relationship, that they tend to deactivate or explain away emotions, and that they are much more comfortable discussing thoughts than feelings.

This stems from a bias toward the logical left hemisphere of the brain. The Security Guard may be able to intellectualize feelings and talk about them without *experiencing* them. An electric fence may keep animals out of the front yard, but it could also prevent a neighbor from bringing over friendship bread. The walls the Security Guard has built up don't discriminate between the joy of intimacy and the pain of conflict.

The Security Guard's experiences of chronic rejection may be associated with a fight-or-flight response, which tends to be associated with activity in the back lower part of the brain. The Security Guard is a pro at masking emotions. When they have a higher cognitive load or are under stress, they must use their resources to think and focus on other things. When that happens, they have less mental and emotional energy to focus on minimizing emotions—which may lead to an emotional eruption (rare for a Security Guard). It's also possible that these emotions will be displaced and come out in other ways, such as road rage. On the journey toward healing, it'll be important to have an active outlet for releasing pent-up emotion and energy with intentionality. Outlets like running may be especially helpful, because they bring the physical into a place that is consistent with what they have done emotionally—run away from connection.

> *The walls the Security Guard has built up don't discriminate between the joy of intimacy and the pain of conflict.*

Understanding the Security Guard

You might be a Security Guard if you've ever said, "I'm going to a party. Do you happen to have any great conversation *stoppers*?" Just like a security guard at a museum keeps people away from exhibits, those with a dismissing and avoidant style have a little inner security guard that says, "Don't let others get too close. Painful things happen when there's a degree of closeness, so distance, space, and independence are a priority."

The Security Guard may feel like their partners encroach on their independence. They say things like, "We don't have to do everything together" or "I just need some time to myself." Security Guards feel one of their most important needs is freedom and independence. They have a large personal bubble, and they value personal space and self-reliance. They have developed these characteristics as coping skills to allow them to survive emotionally desolate environments. They are also more likely to stay on the dating market since they tend to be single more frequently than other relationship styles.

Each relationship style has strengths and utility. Our relationship styles help us survive our early environment, so I don't like to rank any as better than the others. However, some researchers suggest the Security Guard style is the second-most adaptive strategy, after the Networker.[1] Let's look at another example.

Joshua had a Security Guard style. He idealized his relationship partners. He loved the idea of them but not who they actually were. Joshua is not alone. Most Security Guards who indicate they have trouble recalling their past relationship memories idealize their caregivers or partners.[2] You may be wondering why the Security Guard idealizes their partners. It's for the same reason they may report a lack of memory of them, restrict the retelling of a memory by saying their relationship was "just normal," or even disparage a friend who missed their partner at basic training. These are all long-standing strategies of pushing away or setting aside the discussion of *real* relationship or connection.[3] In addition, the Security Guard is often not able to support the positive initial portrayal they present of their caregiver or partner.

We now know this inability comes from the Security Guard being deceived by their own defenses in order to keep painful memories and emotions out of their awareness. This idealization presents a type of cover story that the Security Guard can deem "true enough."[4] It may take the form of unwarranted praise, such as "she was an absolutely wonderful girlfriend," or in the case of caregivers, "he was such an exceedingly wonderful father," with no examples or evidence given to support these claims. This may also fail to line up with reports of lots of rejecting or other unloving behavioral accounts.

When I was working on a research project with other trained coders of a relationship styles assessment called the Adult Attachment Interview, the coders joked that we should give a discount when coding Security Guard interviews because they were almost always shorter than the other styles and took less time to code. In a sense, they were very pleasant to code. However, some strategies used by Security Guards, such as idealization, tended to violate linguists' rules of collaborative discussion—including Grice's supermaxim of quality that suggests we should have evidence of what we say. However, they were overly succinct as they pushed away discussion of their relationship.[5]

Thus, there are two ways that the Security Guard dismisses their relationship partners. The first is to reject them or push them away overtly. The second is to idealize them so that they have a relationship with the idea of their partner rather than their actual partner.

Loving the Security Guard

How do you know if you're in a relationship with a Security Guard? There's one very clear indicator: your partner is clearly moving away from connection. This may feel like rejection.

Let's look at some possible manifestations of this tendency in romantic relationships:

- The predominant response when the Security Guard experiences a loss or setback in life is to turn away. This may mean they go for a run, go to the gym, work longer hours, devote lots of time to their hobby, or spend more time watching television. They might engage in self-care like sitting in the car for long periods of time before coming in after work. Security Guards have multiple ways of withdrawing from their partners to create space.

- The Security Guard may speak highly of you when you aren't around.

- When you start to become vulnerable, they navigate the conversation elsewhere. You wonder if they really love you or if they just love the idea of having a relationship with you (our QTIPs can come in handy once again).

- When you ask your Security Guard about their history or family experiences, there's some sort of block. You find that the conversation goes nowhere fast. They may say they don't remember or would prefer not to talk about it.

- Without work on your behalf, your relationship defaults to two ships passing in the night. You and your Security Guard live as roommates rather than intimate romantic partners.

- The Security Guard only likes to spend time together in certain situations. Perhaps they enjoy having meals together, watching television together, or going to church together, but they don't want to go on walks, go on double dates, or have long conversations about feelings.

You may also notice that things aren't as they appear to be, because the Security Guard is prone to idealizing. For example, you may notice painful tendencies or dysfunction within their family of origin; however, those painful tendencies are never acknowledged. The Security Guard views their caregiver favorably and ignores contradictory evidence. It's as if they are wearing selective sunglasses that dim the light on the truth to make it easier to look at. Or they see what they want to see rather than confront the crudeness of reality. This painful pattern has likely protected them long before they met you.

Here are a few ways the Security Guard's tendencies to turn away from relationships may manifest through different coping styles.

Finding Solace in Stuff

Every professional organizer's number one secret for organization is decluttering. That's the first line of negotiation with clients. They work with them to declutter their world by refreshing and curating their space.

Researchers have found an association between relationship avoidance and the tendency to hoard material objects.[6] Security Guards often seek independence from relationships, but they may find solace in material objects. They may even have elaborate collections of things. Why? Instead of treasured memories of togetherness with *people*, Security Guards focus more on objects or tasks. These items have always been there for them in a way the important people in their lives have not. They hang on to these items that cannot love them back because they provide tangible comfort. This short-term gain can create long-term pain.

Security Guards often seek independence from relationships, but they may find solace in material objects.

While the Security Guard is maximizing objects in their environment, they may also minimize the object of their affection, thereby insulating themselves against their biggest fear: rejection. However, this strategy also protects them from connection and intimacy.

Downplaying Dates

The Security Guard highly values independence and will minimize any degree of needing a relationship by downplaying its importance. Researchers John Bowlby and Mary Ainsworth did a series of studies called "The Strange Situation."[7] In the study, young children were put in a nursery with a stranger while their caregiver was asked to briefly leave the room. Researchers observed the child's behavior when Mom left the room, but they watched the child's behavior even more closely when Mom came back. Bowlby and Ainsworth found that Security Guard children were just as distressed as their Networker and Investigator counterparts at Mom's departure. But as early as three years old, the Security Guards had already learned how to mask their distress and fearful emotions and minimize any signals of needing their caregivers. This behavior helped them deal with their environment because they were faced with a chronically rejecting caregiver. If they sent too much signaling for closeness, they risked further alienating their rejecting caregivers.

If you're in a relationship with a Security Guard, remember they have perfected the process of hiding their emotions. Even children learned to subdue their crying and attempts to pursue their caregivers in an attempt to stay close to them.[8] This default mode developed out of some of their greatest pain and vulnerability. Try to remember the QTIP mindset. In other words, if you can remember that the rejection isn't about you but rather about the Security Guard's own discomfort and pain, their distancing may be less painful and hurtful than if you interpret it as a personal affront.

A Lack of Emotional Intimacy

On the outside it may appear that the Security Guard is calm when their relationship system is activated. The truth is, calmness is often far from them. They've learned to hide their discomfort under the cloak of doubt. Their focus is on independence and self-reliance. They want to dismiss any signals of needing someone else. After all, history has taught them people won't be there for them anyway. They doubt romantic partners' promises. (Unfortunately, this likely extends to their relationship with God as well.[9] They believe they can't count on anyone else to meet their needs, so they may doubt God's goodness too.)

If your partner is a Security Guard, you may find a lack of emotional intimacy from them. It may feel as if they're totally emotionally unavailable and out of touch with their own emotions; likewise, they may also seem unattuned to your emotional needs.

In many cases, the Security Guard received lots of negative feedback or consequences for expressing emotions in their early years. After a lifetime of reacting to these messages, being vulnerable, sharing feelings, and opening up won't come naturally to the Security Guard. These ways of interacting are foreign to them. Though there's a part of them that longs for and needs the same connection as their Networker and Investigator counterparts, it can feel torturously uncomfortable. Humans are creatures of habit. We tend to go for what we know and what we're comfortable with, even if it isn't what's best for us.

One way to help is to proactively utilize your QTIP.[10] If you feel like your partner doesn't miss or need you, it's most likely because they don't. The Security Guard has painstakingly trained themselves to turn away from relationships, to independently deal with their problems and disengage from painful emotions. It is not because there's something wrong with you (as the Investigator and Firefighter may be inclined to think). Please remember this has been part of their wiring since childhood. It isn't personal. Some romantic partners find it helpful to hang on to a baby picture of their partner and imagine them as a child crying and not being answered rather than an unkind rejecting partner.

The Security Guard may also struggle with sharing their emotions. They were taught to overregulate and deactivate (turn off) their emotions and may have a tendency toward intellectualizing. You can model the appropriate expression of emotion in ways that involve being emotionally present without being overwhelming. You could say something like, "Today I felt stressed about all the things that needed to get done, but it felt good to cross things off the list. Now I feel ready to relax and let my hair down." Frequent communication like this may help. For example, if you ask, "How are you feeling?" your Security Guard may respond with, "I feel like I have a lot to do, and I better get to it." This is a thought rather than a feeling, but the Security Guard may not grasp the distinction. Welcome to their world, where thoughts reign supreme and feelings are squelched or minimized. Try to exhibit patience, knowing it is uncomfortable for them to discuss feelings. Pressing can backfire..

If you feel like your partner doesn't miss or need you, it's most likely because they don't.

As you express your emotions in experiential ways, you model appropriate emotional expression. You can also model the link between thoughts, behaviors, and emotions. For example, you may say, "When I think about all I have to do and the little time I have to do it, I feel stressed. I feel a knot in my stomach and my shoulders tighten, and I have a tough time relaxing because I just want to get back to work." It's important to remember that you can't change the Security Guard. In order to have emotional closeness with someone, you need to first know them, and that requires them to share their thoughts. For the Security Guard, this is very hard. Their coping mechanism—avoidance—is like a warm blanket that brings them comfort and familiarity. Avoidance has always been their first line of defense from rejection and other painful experiences.

However, you can *respond well* to the Security Guard in a way that provides the atmosphere for them to grow and get more comfortable with emotions and connection. When the Security Guard makes an effort at connecting, do your best to be responsive and demonstrate acceptance. Try to appreciate the courage it takes for them to risk rejection and make any sort of romantic overture when all their wiring suggests they refrain. They have to lean into the possibility of rejection to reveal themselves and their thoughts and feelings. The Security Guard can begin by coming to terms with the idea that they, too, are an emotional being, despite having denied this part of their experience for much of their life. Psychologists and counselors often recommend that a starting point for this transition to being emotionally present and intelligent involves beginning with carrying a notebook or journal and keeping it with you daily and pausing from time to time to notice how you are feeling. Taking a moment to jot down your thoughts in moments of reflection throughout the day can build a helpful practice of mindfulness and emotional awareness, both of which have many benefits. You can begin with feelings you had in less intense situations separate from your relationship, like work.[11]

Often, we also see that there's something holding the Security Guard back from facing the truth or telling the truth of their relationship story. When you try to have intimate conversations, you may feel like you're doing all the heavy lifting—because you most likely are. The Security Guard's personal narrator is blocked as a safety mechanism, and no amount of prying will help. This is a "you attract more flies with honey" situation: the best you can do is to create a welcoming atmosphere and optimize your responses. It's up to them to determine if and when they're ready to let down their guard.

Here are some simple strategies to keep in mind for loving your Security Guard well:

- Ask them what they need and listen with more than your ears.
- If your Security Guard needs space and time to themselves, give that to them without complaint or taking it personally.
- Avoid relying on your Security Guard for all your relationship needs. It's helpful to have friends in different settings, such as work, church, the gym, and so on, to take the pressure off.
- Consider parallel play: Can you sit in the living room together as you read a book and your Security Guard works on inventorying their coin collection? Try options like this that may meet your need for closeness while honoring their need for space.
- Use what counselors call your "wise mind" (include your intellectual and cognitive experiences as well as your emotions) if you are upset or wanting more connection from your Security Guard. This way your Security Guard is less likely to feel overwhelmed.
- Try modeling your emotional experience in contained ways that transition from intellectual to emotional with subtlety to help reacquaint the Security Guard with emotion. For example, "After our walk in the cool crisp morning air, this cup of tea feels especially warm in my hands, and I can feel it warming me from the inside out!"

- Appreciation is like relationship glue. If you are currently in a relationship with a Security Guard, your Security Guard is leaning into discomfort by having a relationship and negotiating closeness. Try to thank them for any efforts you sense they are making, even if it seems that should not be necessary. And hanging out in Shouldville can keep us stuck.

At the end of the day, your needs and feelings are just as important as your partner's. Remember to ask yourself if your needs are being met in the relationship.

Benefits of the Security Guard's Style

What if you are the Security Guard? First of all, give yourself a pat on the back for picking up this book and being willing to lean into the discomfort of relational awareness! You're undoubtedly aware you tend to be standoffish and you feel uncomfortable when people get too close. You feel like you have to work hard at maintaining your boundaries and your personal space. But human beings are wired for relationships. Your early stance of turning away from relationships kept you safe from the pain of rejection, but now it's also keeping you away from love and true connection.

Dr. Heike Winterheld, a professor at Washington University, led a research project investigating the intentions behind avoidance of emotions in relationships. In short, Dr. Winterheld studied the Security Guard's relationship style because she wanted to take a deeper look at why Security Guards consistently hide their feelings from their loved ones.

Researchers have called this tendency to hide feelings and pretend everything is fine "protective buffering,"[12] and protective buffering is used for two different reasons. Sometimes Security Guards use it to shield their partners from painful emotions. In other cases, Security Guards use it to protect themselves. In either case, the Security Guard aims to keep feelings at bay.

That said, there are benefits to this relationship style.

- The Security Guard has a clear and organized approach to dealing with relationships and emotions.
- The Security Guard is a good *short* storyteller.
- The Security Guard does not get tangled up in relationships or messy, dramatic interpersonal dynamics.
- The Security Guard is likely to have developed their own interests and hobbies, skills, or collections from their time spent independently working or playing.
- You do not have to worry about getting stuck in a long conversation with a Security Guard when you are running late. (Unless you happen upon their favorite interest, such as collecting every US coin in existence or every stamp ever printed in France and all of France's colonies.)
- The Security Guard is likely very resourceful and independent and has probably developed competencies in many areas so as to facilitate their independence and prevent interpersonal rejection.
- The Security Guard will likely be OK with a partner's limited availability and can entertain themselves.
- The Security Guard works well independently and tends to be highly competent.

Though some of the Security Guard's behaviors and tendencies may be off-putting to romantic partners, the Security Guard's style is considered an *organized clear strategy* to deal with relationships. They have a very clear and organized way of dealing with loved ones: they move away and create distance. They can do this physically or emotionally. This clear strategy makes this style more adaptive than a relationship style without clear organization because the Security Guard isn't as likely to get tangled up in relationships.

Optimizing the Security Guard Style

Security Guards won't be ready for a risky journey toward change without first reaching a few conclusions. They must calculate the risk, ensuring they understand the benefits, and be convinced the benefits outweigh the risks. Low-functioning Security Guards who are unwilling to leave their comfort zone will find themselves walking alone for much of life's journey. But how can the Security Guard truly know what they are missing unless they develop a taste for a relationship connection?

Our need for relationships is in a delicate balance. Here's an example: A man who weighs approximately 220 pounds has about 80 teaspoons of salt in his body.[13] Our percentage of saltiness is comparable to that of the ocean's saltwater. We need salt, yet when we exercise, we perspire and lose it; we must replace it continually. We add it to food for flavor, but if we consume too much salt, we can experience problems like high blood pressure. If we have too little, our nerves and muscles will not function correctly.

Likewise, there's a delicate balance in relationships. Like the individual who avoids salt and suffers health consequences, the low-functioning Security Guard has overindulged in avoidant tendencies in relationships to their detriment and suffered the relational consequences. How can the Security Guard lean into the discomfort of closeness or develop a desire to do so?

This taste for connection can be sparked through experiencing the flavor of an intimate relationship, a friendship, or a relationship with God. To embark on this healing journey toward increased security, the Security Guard must be ready to stop playing small and begin writing a new story. It's easy to take a "leap of doubt" when it comes to believing someone won't be there for them. *Awareness* of this tendency is the first step in revising it.

It will take time to revise the Security Guard's relationship blueprint and create a new story. One place to start is with metacognitive monitoring. Self-awareness is considered an important part of some models of emotional intelligence. Self-awareness helps us come to terms with and address areas where lack of awareness can keep us stuck. There are many ways of increasing self-awareness. One way is to ask for feedback from others. Another is journaling. Another is interacting with people who bring out different feelings and thoughts and taking time to reflect on those experiences.

Journaling each day and including a sentence or more on interpersonal experiences and goals can be very helpful.

When warm feelings begin to surface, try to find words for them and express them or write them down. Your partner will likely appreciate your kind words or gesture. It may be uncomfortable to allow these expressions, but it'll make your relationships stronger and safer than if you hold them in. It's important to remember that you developed these avoidant tendencies as a child as a function of thousands of interactions with your environment. They won't change overnight, so please be kind to yourself on this journey.

If you're having trouble expressing your emotions, consider using a feeling wheel. The epitome of emotional intelligence is having the capacity to mention and manage your emotions. If emotions are continuously buried, they'll eventually erupt in unhelpful or even harmful ways, so cultivating an emotionally intelligent approach that allows you to deploy emotions based on their utility is a helpful practice to cultivate. It will increase your capacity to be emotionally present.

The research team I work with at the university where I teach has conducted pilot studies to examine the impact our relationship styles have on our relationship with God. We've also found that relationship style is impacted by the way we view God. When our students participated in God attachment workshops, their tendencies toward avoidance decreased. They participated in activities like worship, mindfulness, reflective prayer, and more.[14]

Dr. Daniel Amen recommends a helpful exercise called "The One Page Miracle"[15] that will help accelerate you down the path toward your goals. I do it personally and also recommend it to all my clients and students. Dr. Amen uses this tool to help people who want to improve their sense of focus or get their life aligned with their goals. In this exercise, you put your goals about the important areas of your life (health, relationships, spirituality, finances, work, education) on one page, then you keep that page in a place where you will see it often. Seeing what you want on paper can help you align your actions with your vision and help you accomplish your goals.

In addition to all the traditional key areas of life, be sure to include special attention to interpersonal relationships on your one page. Create goals in these areas and ask yourself regularly, "Am I moving toward these goals? If my goal is to have a strong relationship, am I taking time to be a good partner?"

A Neighborly Exercise to Increase Security

If you experienced a lot of rejection in childhood, you're in good company. Fred Rogers, host of *Mister Rogers' Neighborhood*, was bullied and frequently ill as a child. He spent a lot of time in his room entertaining himself with puppets. However, he received a healing message from his grandpa who used to tell him, "Freddy, you have made this day a special day just by your being you. There is no one in the whole world like you, and I like you just the way you are."[16]

This meant so much to young Freddy that, years later, he paid this message forward by sharing it with children across the United States and Canada in nearly every episode of his program. He also helped others learn a technique to magnify their healing experiences. Or as the apostle Matthew writes: "Let me tell you why you are here. You're here to be salt-seasoning that brings out the God-flavors of this earth" (Matt. 5:13 MSG).

Mister Rogers wanted to inspire people to make goodness attractive and to make room for reflection. One of the ways he did that was by acknowledging that we have each arrived where we are in our lives because there were people who cared about us. The Security Guard may feel as if they have built their life on their own, but as they search their memories, they may be reminded of teachers, mentors, coaches, or others who nurtured their development.

Don't laugh, Security Guard—I know the kind-caring-feeling–oriented nature of Mister Rogers may seem the antithesis of how you were socialized, but one of my colleagues, Dr. Kevin Hull, told me that *Mister Rogers' Neighborhood* taught him he could be masculine *and* express his feelings. Emotional intelligence may seem elusive and even undesirable to the Security Guard, but I encourage learning more about Mister Rogers's message about human relations. I recommend starting with the documentary of his life, *Won't You Be My Neighbor?* Even though he is gone, Mister Rogers can help with priming or be a mentor/parental figure of sorts. The warmth and expressions of care he offered are consistent with the safe haven messages we need from our most important relationships. Do you have young children? This may be a great opportunity to help them cultivate emotional intelligence; sitting down to watch and discuss the program with them could be life-changing.

Other Strategies for Revising the Narrative

Consider journaling. Think about your most important interpersonal relationships. What are your interpersonal goals? For example, "I'd like to have a marriage that's emotionally, intellectually, spiritually, and physically intimate." If this is your goal, what do you need to do to accomplish it? Are you doing those things? You need to ask yourself, "Am I sharing my emotions, thoughts, spiritual experiences, and affections with my partner regularly?"

Reading can also help. Let me recommend *The Blessing* by John Trent and Gary Smalley; *Feeling Good Together* by David Burns; and *The 5 Love Languages* by Gary Chapman. And don't forget to add *Won't You Be My Neighbor?* to your watch list.

KEY TAKEAWAYS

- The Security Guard has used avoidance to avoid the risk of rejection.
- The Security Guard may enjoy time alone. They value independence and self-reliance.
- The Security Guard may not be in touch with their own needs or emotions and is likely to minimize and avoid emotions.
- The Security Guard style has some benefits, such as a clear approach to relationships, the ability to be concise, the absence of relational drama, and high levels of independence.
- Partners of the Security Guard do well to honor the Security Guard's request for space. They should avoid pressuring the Security Guard to conform to their desire for connection and intimacy prematurely, as this could backfire.

A CONCEPT TO CONTEMPLATE

What ideas or expectations do you have of your current or future romantic partner? How may these expectations be different from or similar to reality with that partner? Write these thoughts in your journal. Think about how you might use any insights in a way that benefits both of you.

Love is patient and kind; love does not envy or boast; it is not arrogant or rude. It does not insist on its own way; it is not irritable or resentful; it does not rejoice at wrongdoing, but rejoices with the truth. Love bears all things, believes all things, hopes all things, endures all things.

1 Corinthians 13:4–7 ESV

7

The Networker

I always admired my Mims. She was about eightyish years young when I began to wonder how she seemed to make everyone around her sweeter and kinder. She was a pro at bringing out the best in people, even the grumpiest curmudgeon. I wanted to learn her ways, so I started to study her more closely. One of the first things I noticed was her contagious enthusiasm and her pleasantly effusive nature. She would pat, rest her hand on, hug, kiss, or squeeze her loved ones. She generously assigned terms of endearment; sweet girl, sweetheart, and honey were some of her favorites for me.

So, one day I decided to express my appreciation to her. "Mims, I love the way you use terms of endearment for everyone! It seems to just bring out their sweet side."

She leaned toward me. "Can I tell you something, honey?" she asked.

"Tell me something, Mims," I replied, leaning in close too.

"It's so I don't have to remember their names," she confessed.

Dr. Ida Molina-Zinam, aka Mims, satisfactorily smiling like she got away with something, like not remembering names for years, with none of us noticing or minding a bit.

Through all the years Mims graced my life, she was a widow. In her lifetime, she buried two of her four sons and her only daughter. Despite these hardships, her loving nature and valuing of relationships remained intact; she was one of the most loving people I ever knew, and admiring her ways gave me eyes to see and ears to hear loving behaviors in my environment. Courtesy of Mims, I noticed the love of a couple who share characteristics of classic Networkers. Their names are Dave and Donna, but you may know them as the Dancing Duo.[1]

A Look at Networkers: The Dancing Duo

In the city of Roanoke, Virginia, you can find a couple inviting others to join them on the dance floor. The beat of the music pulsates and the lyrics, "'Cause Uptown Funk gon' give it to you,"[2] echo in the speakers. This couple made their state's travel slogan some of America's truest words: Virginia is for lovers. Here's their backstory.

A graceful ballroom dancer, Donna was a woman with flawless skin, chocolate brown eyes, and a captivating smile. Even more beautiful than her outward appearance was her unmistakably and authentically kind disposition. Donna was, as happily married women often are, pursued by her partner. When I asked Donna how she met the love of her life, she told me it all began with an accident.

Donna was single and Dave was single again, but it wasn't until a fender bender brought her into Dave's place of work that their paths crossed for the first time. Dave was tall and had thick wavy brown hair and a winning smile. He was a friend to many. The two hit it off. Dave proposed to Donna on a large billboard in Roanoke. Soon after, another billboard followed with the fresh declaration: "She said yes!"

As you may have guessed by their nickname, the Dancing Duo, Dave and Donna are popular ballroom dancers. If you have lived in Roanoke, Virginia, for a while, you may have also seen a billboard that Dave thoughtfully put up as a birthday gift for Donna back in 2001. Dave wrote the catchy caption: "You are the best thing that ever danced into my life. Love, Dave."

The Dancing Duo welcomed me to the world of ballroom dancing in Roanoke when I met them at a ballroom dance event, and I have admired their special connection since. They graciously gave me permission to share their story. One of the first things I noticed about them was not only their ability to glide across the dance floor so gracefully but also their constant use of terms of endearment to refer to each other. There's a tenderness in their communication with one another; the emotional tone they use with one another lets you know her name is safe in his mouth and vice versa.

Dave and Donna celebrate not only anniversaries but sometimes monthiversaries too. They got married in their fifties and decided to celebrate their relationship as much as possible while they can. Yet they are not immune to conflict. It is a part of their experience, just like any other couple. When I asked how they navigate the rougher waters, Donna shared their secret.

They get through tough times because Dave and Donna each believe they're a gift from God to the other. This kind of valuing—not only believing the other is a gift from God but remembering this and treating the other as such—is part of the relationship style of the Networker. Dave and Donna value each other highly. Donna says that when they have a disagreement, they try to sit down and talk about it. They each want to know and hear how the other person feels. Dave and Donna clearly move toward each other, and they're comfortable connecting emotionally and sharing feelings.

The Networker's Origin Story

Networkers tend to have low anxiety about relationships and low avoidance levels. This means they have high levels of comfort with closeness and peace, comfort, and security with their relationships. Since Networkers are comfortable with emotional intimacy, they tend to move straight toward it. It is important to note that within each relationship style, people may be higher or lower functioning along a continuum. Some Networkers may have a wee bit more anxiety or avoidance than others; likewise, other Networkers may have a morsel more of avoidance.

Networkers are connectors because they have a capacity to turn toward others and readily trust, as well as give and receive care. They believe they're worthy of love and that others are able to show them love, making it easier for them to have the courage to be vulnerable. In childhood, when the Networker ran to Mom with a skinned knee after crashing their bike, they knew a kiss was coming "to make it better." (Even though they were not supposed to be riding their bike without supervision, they did not fear reprimand because they knew any reprimand came from a place of love.) Alone in bed and suddenly frightened by nighttime sounds, they would cry out—knowing a comforting hand and gentle forehead kiss were coming soon, along with the careful inspection for monsters under the bed, the whisper of "no monsters found here," and the loving tuck of the covers.

The Networker knew and trusted love was coming for them and was quickly comforted during times of distress. Thus, their experiences learning they could depend on trustworthy caregivers grew in number, and with the growth of those experiences, their security grew as well.

In romantic attachment, Networkers have the capacity to depend on their partner because their history taught them to trust and to feel secure with others. For example, when Dave and Donna hit patches of conflict, they sit down together to listen and find out what the other person is thinking and feeling. Networkers can count on their partner to be there for them emotionally and to help them make sense of their feelings (just as their caregivers did for them).

Networkers are able to express their needs freely and clearly. While teaching dance class, Dave and Donna would often ask the other to help them demonstrate a move or to switch roles and would accompany their request with a sweet smile or term of endearment. Both parties shared their needs and affections freely.

The Networker's Relationship Blueprint

The Networker's relationship blueprint is very simple: the answers to our two questions—*Am I worthy of love?* and *Can others be counted on to love me?*—are a resounding yes and yes.

This sets them up for success in future relationships. They have an advantage. It is easier to build trust with partners, because their history has taught them others are trustworthy and can be counted on to meet their needs. Moving toward their loved ones during times of distress comes naturally for them, and they feel comfortable expressing, missing, and needing. It is easier for them to calm down if they get upset with their partner, and they are often very at ease both giving and receiving comfort.

Because they learned how to internalize a kind caregiver long ago, Networkers have an internal kind caregiver they can use to self-soothe and care for themselves, even as adults. This allows them to respond with more compassion toward themselves and their relationship partners. They are not looking to romantic partners to compensate for love they never got growing up; they tend to be balanced in their view and have their sense of humor intact. When you ask them about their relationship histories (including familial and romantic), they often have vivid and cogent stories to tell.

Networkers are much less likely to be available on the dating market since they tend to stay in couplings—connecting deeply and valuing their partners highly. When people with other relationship styles get romantically involved with a prototypical high-functioning Networker, they may feel like they have only seen a shadow of what a relationship could be! The Networker can reassure the Investigator they are worthy of love, and their compassionate nature can help the Investigator's relationship anxiety melt away. Likewise, the Networker can respect the Security Guard's need for space without taking it personally, helping the Security Guard relinquish the need to guard their walls firmly. The Networker also has a knack for reassuring the Firefighter that they are *both* worthy of love and able to love. Networkers want to get to know their partner and pursue true intimacy—without makeup, pretension, or the other masks we wear.

It is also easier for the Networker to have a vibrant relationship with God. They are not immune to tragedy and may even question their faith when difficult things happen, but they are more likely to go to God with their questions and hold fast to their faith because of the deep roots of trust that come from the resounding yeses wired in to their internal relationship blueprint.

Understanding the Networker

The Networker has had one of two experiences that make trust and connection possible: (1) a host of experiences that taught them others can and will love them or (2) an emotionally corrective experience that made sense of painful moments with others and exemplified how others can love them and how they are worthy of love.

When facing distress, the Networker turns *toward* their relationship partner and is quickly soothed and reassured. As Dr. John Gottman and his colleagues found in a now-famous experiment on romantic relationships, *turning toward* is part of the seven principles to making marriage work.[3] Gottman's seven principles seem unambiguous when you think about them:

1. Share likes and dislikes.
2. Nurture fondness and admiration.
3. Turn toward your partner instead of away.
4. Let your partner influence you.
5. Solve the solvable problems.
6. Overcome gridlock.
7. Create a shared sense of meaning.[4]

Yet our relationship styles greatly influence our capacity to fulfill these principles, especially our capacity to turn toward our partner during times of distress.

The Networker values relationships and is prepared to invest time and resources to make them work. In the heat of the moment, when couples disagree, it is not easy to sit down and calmly listen and understand someone else. It is not easy to "give up your right to be understood" for the sake of understanding someone else, as my mentor (a prototypical Networker) Dr. J. used to advise as a necessary skill. However, it is a good investment of time and emotional resources.

Networkers also freely express emotions like missing, needing, and valuing. We can see this communication between Dave and Donna. Communication of high-valuing comments—"we think of each other as a gift from God"—is also commonplace in the Networker's correspondence.

The Networker not only values, misses, and needs important relationship partners but is also able to depend on them and be depended upon by them. They are comfortable getting close, whether in a ballroom dance setting or in deep conversations about meaning and values.

Thinking about Your Thinking

The Networker often communicates in ways that may be unique from other relationship styles, because they are naturally skilled at metacognitive monitoring. Because of this awareness of their thoughts, when the Networker shares their story, there seems to be a degree of freshness and presence that's captivating. Networkers may even pause to think about their thinking. For example, they may say, "I'm trying to come up with a memory of how our relationship was extremely loving, but I keep thinking of memories of just basic parenting!" This self-awareness and capacity to reflect on their thinking in the moment keeps the narrative fresh and lively. If you are interacting with a Networker, you may also come away with a feeling of connection, such as, "She talked to me as if I was the only person in the world." We don't often see examples of canned speech in the interpersonal narrative of a Networker. This is just one of the features of their way of thinking and talking about relationships that sets them apart. They are also often more emotionally calm since their relationships have been full of support; they do not carry extra worry with them. Their balance and humor also often help them contribute to a positive emotional climate in their relationships.

The Quality of the Narrator

There's something about the way the Networker tells their relationship story that draws people in. When I interview a Networker, there are strong themes of appreciating relationships—it's a cooperative dialogue. If I ask a Networker a question, a relevant, cogent, and clear-sighted answer typically follows.

Although in many cases the Networker has had positive childhood experiences, there are some exceptions to this rule. If a child has challenging experiences with their caregivers but is able to make sense of those experiences and meaningfully weave them into their larger relationship story, they can still manifest the Networker's style. These clear and coherent ways of communicating tend to be true for the Networker, whether or not their retrospective childhood experiences with caregivers were positive or negative.

This is one of the hopeful and promising things about relationship styles: it isn't the experiences themselves that matter most but how you *think* about them when it comes to your relationship style. How you think about your interpersonal history is revealed in the manner in which you talk about your experiences and share your relationship story.[5]

Moving Toward

One main feature of the Networker's style is clearly moving toward connection. If we think of each style on a linear path, Networkers move toward each other. Security Guards do the opposite of Networkers and move away from relationship. Investigators get turned around and tangled up on the journey and wind up on a more circuitous path. And Firefighters have no clear predictable movement.

Some researchers have created "the Close Scale," which measures comfort with closeness in romantic relationships. They found this comfort was related to some key childhood experiences that Networkers tend to have that are different from other relationship style experiences. Some relationship style tests assess the level of loving experiences or neglect with Mom during childhood and pressure to achieve from Dad.[6] Surprisingly, though pressure to achieve is often considered an unloving experience, some studies see it as a father's way of being involved and encouraging growth. If a person was comfortable with closeness in romantic relationships, they also tended to be able to narrate their story in a coherent and cooperative way.[7]

Networkers also tend to be able to comfortably depend on their romantic partners. Research shows they have had:

- loving experiences with Mom that go above and beyond the basic needs for food, shelter, clothing, and transportation to school
- the opportunity to be the child rather than the caregiver; didn't have to take care of their caregiver's emotional needs
- lower levels of neglect from Mom than other relationship styles
- lower likelihood of experiencing rejection and neglect from Dad than other relationship styles

When it comes to the Networker's state of mind, certain mindsets and ways of thinking set them apart from the other relationship styles:

- low levels of anger with Mom
- low to no lingering anger toward Dad (in most cases)
- no lack of memory or blocking when it comes to discussing their childhood experiences (Even if those experiences were painful or negative, they've found a way to make sense of them within the larger narrative of their relationship story.)
- ability to articulate when telling their stories (They tend to be able to share experiences in a vivid way without vague expressions that leave listeners wondering what they mean. Researchers call this vague language *passive speech*.)
- joy at the opportunity to tell their relationship story, exhibiting high levels of coherence

Loving the Networker

If your partner is a Networker, I have some good news for you. In romantic relationships, Networkers are comfortable expressing their needs and are open to hearing yours, as we saw with the Dancing Duo. This doesn't mean that Networkers won't go through heartaches, divorces, breakups, or other separations, but it does mean their comfort with valuing and needing will make their relationships more satisfying.

One place to start the journey to an even more secure Networking style is knowing your needs, emotions, and values so you can communicate them clearly to your partner. That's why the "A Concept to Contemplate" sections are so important. We will talk more about strategies for optimizing your relationship style in chapter 8.

The Background of the Networker

In childhood, Networkers tended to hear the words "I love you" or have them communicated one way or another on a regular basis. In adulthood, they may feel comfortable being effusive. You may hear Networkers saying things to each other like, "You sure are lucky you're cute," "I love you to the moon and back," or any other unique expression of "I love you," "I need you," and/or "I miss you" with great comfort and creativity. Like my Mims, Networkers are generous with terms of endearment and may call loved ones "honey," "sweetie," or "sugar."

The point is the Networker is comfortable with closeness and affection, and they value relationships. This may be communicated in a number of creative linguistic manifestations or even silently by bringing a partner a shopping cart at the store. Affection, closeness, and turning toward are the name of the game for the Networker. They are comfortable talking about both the good and the bad and may be able to "sugar," "sweetie," and "honey" their partner while delivering a request for change. For example, the Networker may deliver a honey-do list like so: "Sugar, would you please take out the trash and empty the dishwasher? I know you didn't get to it because you were tired yesterday." The Networker keeps a balanced perspective most of the time.

The Networker also understands human nature, that we are creatures of choice and can choose love. It can be challenging to love when relationship partners act unlovely, yet persons of faith have a role model who sets the bar high for true love—what some authors have called "love's greatest challenge"[8]: "But to you who are listening I say: Love your enemies, do good to those who hate you, bless those who curse you, pray for those who mistreat you. . . . If you love those who love you, what credit is that to you? Even sinners love those who love them" (Luke 6:27–28, 32).

Clients have sometimes asked me about the thin line between love and hate in relationships. They've also asked why their partner has such an unloving way of showing love. Even if they're in a relationship with a relationally savvy Networker, people with the other relationship styles are likely to ask these questions. It is easy for the Investigator to feel that their Networker partner hates them, because the Investigator believes they are not worthy of love. Likewise, it is not a tough leap of doubt for the Security Guard to doubt their Networker partner's love and to create distance to safeguard their heart and salvage their independence. In long-term relationships, people with different relationship styles (even the emotionally intelligent Networker) can begin to feel like their relationship partners hate them when love tanks get low and love fades, as often happens in the grind of daily life. The Networker's history has taught them that partners do not abandon ship when things get tough but rather find ways to weather the storm, even if it means sacrificing and suffering for a season. For many, it may start with taking the initiative to work on the relationship, while their partner may not be matching their effort. However, the law of reciprocity suggests that eventually what you give will come back to you in some way, shape, or form. Psychologists and counselors often find that once one partner's love tank is filled, they have more emotional assets to meet their partner's needs.

Often, if we don't intentionally change our ways of relating to important relationships in childhood, those models will follow us into adult romantic relationships. That's usually good news for the Networker; they tend to wholeheartedly believe they can depend on their romantic partners. They're also more likely to feel more comfortable with intimacy in romantic relationships, which builds trust in another who may not do so easily.

One reason the Networker may be able to make sense of both their fulfilling and difficult interpersonal experiences is their strength with metacognition; they tend to be comfortable in their relationships, low in relationship anxiety, high in comfort with closeness, and thus more able to be mentally present in the moment. Their aptitude to freely narrate their feelings and relationship experiences is an asset that helps them roll with the relational punches.

Benefits of the Networker's Style

Why does having an adaptive relationship style matter? This is where the strengths and struggles of the Networker's style are revealed, including the rewards of a rich and close-knit social network and support system. However, there are costs to loving well, including experiencing grief more deeply after a loss.

There are costs to loving well, including experiencing grief more deeply after a loss.

The Networker is the most adaptive of the relationship styles. They have the greatest advantages in relationships and are most likely to experience happy, long-lasting, fulfilling relationships. Networkers also have the most to lose; as with their propensity to highly value their relationships, they are hardest hit by losses. However, having an insecure or less adaptive relationship style is even more costly—and there are both financial[9] and physical costs in addition to emotional and relational costs.[10]

The good news is an adaptive relationship style like the Networker's has been linked to a long list of benefits.[11] As you contemplate the long journey toward optimizing your relationship style, take a look at the benefits package that comes along with the Networker's style.

Researchers have found that "secure attachment states of mind have been related to outcomes ranging from social competence with peers, constructive regulation of emotion during tasks with spouses and higher romantic relationship quality, as well as inversely related to depressive symptoms and externalizing behavior."[12] Here are more benefits:

- Networkers are more likely to survive a major health condition like cancer.[13]
- Networkers incur fewer health care costs and are less likely to report clinically significant symptoms.[14]
- Networkers tend to have higher levels of existential meaning and purpose.[15]
- Networkers have higher interpersonal expectations than those with insecure styles.[16]
- Networkers tend to dodge problems with low self-esteem experienced by those with other relationship styles.[17]
- Networkers often have significantly fewer symptoms of low mood than other styles.[18]

Emotions and the Networker

An important part of any relationship is emotional connection. As we develop relationship styles during childhood, we tend to forge an innate strategy for dealing with emotions. Let's look at how the Networker tends to deal with emotions:

- Networkers are comfortable with intimacy. Getting scolded, bashed, or insulted by a Networker for sharing vulnerable emotions or needs is not something their partners need to worry about.
- Networkers express a full range of emotions both pleasant and unpleasant without exaggerating the pleasant or minimizing the unpleasant.
- Networkers' emotional expression allows for greater levels of intimacy in relationships. As they become comfortable with their own feelings and needs, they're better able to express them.
- Networkers understand the value of emotions, appreciating that emotions communicate something important. For example, sadness can communicate that we lost

someone or something that was important to us. Anger can convey an injustice or that we've been blocked from something we want.

- Networkers aren't overwhelmed by emotions. They're typically able to communicate and own thoughts and emotions in ways that don't overwhelm others. Self-revelation is their strong suit, making it easy to make themselves known and set an example for others to do the same, facilitating courteous connection.

- Since Networkers move toward emotions, they do not hold anger in and wait for it to become hatred or spew anger in a way that is hurtful to their partner. Instead, they learn to express their feelings in productive ways that do not hurt themselves or others. This tendency to understand, express, and share emotions while moving toward relationship allows Networkers to connect easily with others.

- Networkers tend to be emotionally available, present, laser-focused, and keen on connecting.

The Networker's Faith

Some Networkers experience a close spiritual relationship with God. In the Bible, people interacted with God in very relational ways. Some called him "Father," "Abba," "heavenly Father," and even "Lover of my soul."

Here's how one king with the Networker's style navigated his spiritual relationship when his relationship system was highly activated.

When King David returned home from battle, he found his home had been burned to the ground. He and his men's wives, sons, and daughters had all been taken captive. What was David's response? David and those with him wept, and they didn't stop until they had no more strength to weep.

Then David turned to his safe haven. (The story is recounted in 1 Samuel 30.)

Let's keep the Circle of Security (see chap. 2) in mind as we revisit David's story. David was on the bottom side of the circle and needed safety. Like a classic Networker, he turned toward his ultimate relationship figure, his first love. For him, that was God, his heavenly Father: "But David strengthened himself in the LORD his God" (1 Sam. 30:6 ESV).

David asked for the ephod, a priestly garment, and went straight to his God. He needed to decide if he was going to pursue the troops who had captured his people and wanted to know if he would overtake them. The Lord gave David affirmation. Ultimately, David led his troops to attack from dawn to dusk and recovered everything he had lost, plus some. His story with God was characterized by turning toward Him, seeking Him, and finding answers in Him. These practices taught David that God would be there for him. He was able to share his needs and distress and receive comfort.

This is often the experience of the Networker. They are quick to trust and believe their relationship figures will be there for them in times of distress.

Optimizing the Networker Relationship Style

You may be wondering if there's any hope if you are *not* currently resonating with the Networker's style. The answer is yes! Throughout this book, I've emphasized that you're not stuck (though it may feel like it) with your current relationship style. Whatever style you currently identify with on the test, you can optimize and increase to a higher-functioning Firefighter, Investigator, or Security Guard. You can think of this process as optimizing your relationship style, becoming a high-functioning version of your style, or moving toward greater security. Scholars in relationship research tend to call this process "earning security." As you optimize your style, you can eventually move from an insecure style to a more secure style. Each style is on a continuum, so you can become a secure version of your style with lower levels of relationship avoidance or anxiety. The more secure you become, the lower the anxiety and avoidance you experience and the more adaptive and resilient your relationships are likely to become. Some researchers even indicate that relationship style change could be an outcome of counseling.[19]

Sometimes a child has grown up with caregivers who weren't always available. That person may intentionally look to other relationships to have needs met. For example, a client I'll call Roberto moved to the United States from Mexico. His parents didn't speak English, but he quickly learned English, so he was able to help them acclimate. At the same time, Roberto's soccer coach helped him adjust to life in the States. He looked to his coach and his friends' fathers for guidance more than his own parents during his developmental years.

One subtype of the secure style involves being a Networker at heart with some Security Guard tendencies. In other words, you value relationships but you recognize, for some reason, that your caregivers can't provide the responsive care you need. Maybe your mother had you when she was a teen or your parents struggled with mental health problems, addictions, or alcoholism. You still value and love them but you turn away a bit from them.

Thus, in your turning away you turn toward other relationship figures. Maybe a teacher, an aunt or uncle, the parent of a friend, a sports coach, or a grandparent is able to help you by providing the love and support you need to develop the relationship beliefs that you're worthy of love. Perhaps they demonstrate that there are others with the resources and abilities to show you love. Each of the other styles can become more secure as they move on the continuum from relationship anxiety and avoidance to revising those relationship beliefs in the affirmative.

The Networker's Style and the Brain

Relationship styles are activated when we experience distress. The Networker does not have to slowly warm to the idea that it is OK to trust people or to trust against their better judgment (which is the case for the Security Guard). The Networker's history has taught them—and their discernment tells them more often than not—that most people can be reasonably counted upon to meet their needs. They have experienced responsive caregivers, and they tend to believe people will be there to support them, so they move toward connection.

This can mean Networkers experience more physical touch and the benefit of the oxytocin that is its by-product. There are some differences on a neural level. The Networker's brain looks a bit different from the other styles. They have greater neural integration, meaning they have access to a wide range of neural circuitry. They can shift neural gears when needed. In other words, the brain's gearshift, their anterior cingulate gyrus, tends to work extremely well. They rarely get stuck holding grudges or ruminating on negative thoughts. If they do have some of these thoughts, their prefrontal cortex (PFC) is accessible to regulate the thought and move them toward connection.

One function of the PFC is to redirect unhelpful thoughts when they emerge. It is associated with goal-directed behavior. Some call this emotional maturity, emotional intelligence, affective maturity, self-control, or, simply, discipline. In practice this involves being able to recognize, name, and understand the value or utility of an emotion, and it also involves being able to use our attentional deployment to attend to emotions for their utility without exaggerating or minimizing them. This is all part of emotional intelligence. In the Bible, Queen Esther's careful planning—making a special meal and bringing up a topic of concern to her king—is a great example of an emotionally intelligent approach to addressing a relational concern.

When it comes to emotional intelligence, we can take a more scientific look at emotion regulation; researchers have described it as both a culminating skill or ability we can develop and a trait we can grow to possess. Researchers who think of emotional intelligence as an ability have found it comes at the top of a cumulative hierarchy, where a person must first be able to master three other prerequisites: (1) recognize emotions in facial expressions, (2) be able to use emotions to facilitate thinking, and (3) be able to understand emotional messages. Only after mastering these feats can a person manage emotions in the self and others.

Another popular model of emotional intelligence evaluates it as a set of fifteen traits. Emotion regulation is a part of the emotional intelligence traits termed *self-control* and is grouped with traits like low impulsivity and stress management. A pilot study with my founding research team members Dorel Captari and John Harrichand found that while studying counselors-in-training, the higher their emotion regulation traits, the less counselor burnout and emotional exhaustion they experienced.[20]

Networkers have an advantage when it comes to emotion regulation. Relationship science researchers have found that the ability to master and manage emotions is closely linked with relationship systems. Early in life, Networkers learned to manage their emotions by seeking closeness to caregivers, and depending on their reliability and responsiveness, the Networker received comfort and care. Eventually those children were able to internalize models of their caregivers and provide that comfort and care to calm themselves and others when upset. As the Networkers' positive experiences with their caregivers grow, so does their own emotional intelligence. Thus, relationship science researchers have gone so far as to say that relationship styles serve the function of managing emotion.

Networkers tend to have the capacity to be less preoccupied with worries about their relationships. They use their attuned right brain to attend to their emotions as well as their logical left. Adult Networkers may find it easier to be fully present and responsive to partners given their wiring.

The ability to master and manage emotions is closely linked with relationship systems.

Networkers also have access to the logical left brain to comprehend those emotions using Wernicke's region—the area of the brain where the motor neurons are located, which directs both speech and language. On the left, Networkers also have access to Broca's area—often called the brain's scriptwriter—which helps them understand part of *why* they're able to put together their thoughts in a collaborative and coherent manner.[21]

Since Networkers experience more neural integration, they're able to integrate both the emotions associated with their experiences and the words to describe them.[22] This requires much of the brain circuitry to work together.

Of course, the Networker can experience things that are harmful to their brain—such as a concussion, exposure to toxins, or anything else that's detrimental to brain health. However, their nurturing environment does tend to give them a leg up. Those who have walked through trauma, chronic interpersonal insults, or chronic rejection—as some of the other relationship styles have—often struggle to communicate in this same manner.

So it's important to remember that even though Networkers may be masterful storytellers, they aren't immune to grief, loss, and trauma. But the Networker tends to have higher levels of what Daniel Amen calls "brain reserve," which is like an additional layer of cushioning around the brain.[23] When faced with these obstacles and various life stressors, brain reserve contributes to a higher level of resilience and increases a person's capacity to bounce back from interpersonal challenges.

The Networker typically has access to a wide array of neural circuitry, and with it, they can more often run things from the top down rather than operating from the bottom up, which is common when a person is in a state of emergency. Most Networkers started developing their emotional intelligence as babies in their birthday suits; they were quickly and constantly comforted by a calm, collected caregiver.

It is one thing to be a Networker high in emotional intelligence from birth, but to develop the security of a Networker with the background of a Security Guard, Investigator, or Firefighter requires intentionality and hard work—in or out of the birthday suit. It requires the courage to come to terms with one's past and even to wade around in the pain of their difficult experiences and memories. This is no easy feat.

The Networker's Adult Romantic Relationships

Ideally, for romantic relationships, you'd already be well on your journey to optimizing your relationship style and becoming more secure, and your partner would be doing the same. As Dr. Gary Sibcy likes to say, "In this imperfect world, we actually have to tell people how we feel and what we want or don't want. Otherwise, they just won't get it. And even when we do tell them, they may not respond the way they should."[24]

If you're a Networker and in a relationship with someone with a more insecure relationship style, all is not lost. As you develop enhanced security within your own style, you'll find that the changes you make can influence other relationship dynamics. It's important to remember that here in Realville, we can't change anyone except ourselves. However, we can *influence* others. We can learn to love well and bring understanding and empathy for our partner's relationship blueprints into our relationships while also advocating for our own needs.

It's also important to remember that one person can't meet *all* of your relationship needs. We were built for community. Becoming a Networker involves working to build your network of important relationships, which can be quite a challenge in our social media–bound, electronic, remote-working, disconnected, post-COVID society. However, with the right strategies, it is doable.

Remember . . .

The brain is malleable. Traits associated with the Networker's style—metacognition, emotional intelligence, emotion regulation, forgiveness, balanced perspective, humor—can be developed when life offers opportunities for emotionally corrective experiences. Networkers may not have started out as Networkers, but someone somewhere along the journey taught them what love is. Life does provide second chances and opportunities to start on the path to more secure relationships.[25]

KEY TAKEAWAYS

- The Networker is a master connector who moves toward relationship closeness.
- The Networker is comfortable connecting emotionally and expressing a range of emotions.
- The Networker is the most secure optimized style.
- The Networker is low in both attachment anxiety and avoidance.

- The Networker is a pro at self-revelation; they relish sharing their thoughts and feelings with clarity and can help their relationship partners do the same, lending to enhanced emotional intimacy.

A CONCEPT TO CONTEMPLATE

Our relationship rules originate in childhood with our first family or caregiver relationships. Whether you had rejecting experiences with your caregivers, ongoing experiences with difficult caregivers, or relatively responsive relationships with caregivers who provided sensitive and consistent support, at some point all relationships are interrupted—whether by death, divorce, moving away, or another type of separation. As you get out your journal, think about this: If you were to find yourself separated from one of your loved ones or someone you are in an important relationship with, what would you do? What coping strategies do you have in your tool kit?

> The LORD is my shepherd; I shall not want.
> He makes me lie down in green pastures.
> He leads me beside still waters.
> He restores my soul.
> He leads me in paths of righteousness
> for his name's sake.
>
> Psalms 23:1–3 ESV

8

The Path to Connection

Clive Staples Lewis (better known as C. S. Lewis) was a renowned Irish-born, English-bred author and Christian apologist. He wrote dozens of books, including the widely acclaimed fantasy series The Chronicles of Narnia. Despite his popularity, it was not until later in his life that Lewis found joy—Joy Davidman, that is. He married the American poet at the tender age of fifty-eight. Sadly, she died of cancer four years after they were wed. However, those years taught him many things, not the least of which included important lessons on love and loss. Clive and Joy were of two very different schools of thought. He was reserved and bookish. She was outgoing and uninhibited. However, they each offered the other new ways of seeing old things.

In *Shadowlands*, a film that portrays their relationship, there's a poignant scene that unveils a powerful truth about love and loss. Joy wants to talk with Lewis about the end of her life (as any Networker would), but he doesn't want to talk about it (as any Security Guard wouldn't). He just wants to focus on enjoying the moments they have in the present.

But Joy is insistent. She reminds him of an important truth: the pain that comes after your loved one dies is part of the joy of the love shared now. Pain is the price of love.

Joy was right.

The Journey toward Security

When I was going through my training in the science of attachment, I met a colleague from Holland who'd spent much of her life coding relationship style tests for her husband's therapy clients. As we discussed the three insecure relationship styles (the Firefighter, the Investigator, and the Security Guard) compared with the secure style (the Networker), we found one primary difference that separated the insecure styles from the secure. Networkers have learned one lesson that those with an insecure style have not: *what love is*. Those with an insecure style haven't truly grasped what love is.

In my clinical training, I remember learning that one method of experiencing rejection included a child being "spoiled" with gifts. I remember asking my professor if they'd read the *The 5 Love Languages*, which mentions that receiving gifts is a language of love. I was sharply reprimanded. My professor explained that gifts can be a substitute for other, truer forms of love, like when a divorced parent sends gifts but fails to show up. If a person had few loving experiences other than receiving gifts, they came to associate love with material items.

Let's look at how this lesson (being taught what love is) manifests in self-talk or thinking about the concept of love and relationships. If we had to identify a catchphrase for each style, we might consider the following:

Firefighter: Why love and risk the pain of rejection? And what if I'm flawed and can't be loved anyway? Would anyone love me if they really knew me? We all seem to have so many issues. So much can go wrong. What's the point?

Investigator: I want love more than anything, but it always seems to elude me. Maybe there's something wrong with me. If I can just be good enough, maybe I can find someone who will love me.

Security Guard: What's the point of loving when it can hurt so darn much when things end? There's so much at risk. No thanks. I will keep my independence.

Networker: As Tennyson said, "Better to have loved and lost than never to have loved at all."

It's important to remember that these beliefs have helped each style survive the relational cards they've been dealt since childhood. Even if they didn't start with the most adaptive and secure style, the style the child developed served them and helped them navigate the environments they faced.

So the journey from a lonely history to security is a gift! Consider the secure Networker style and the predictive validity of earned security for other relationship styles.

Researchers have studied a relationship style known as "earned secure."[1] They have found that some people grow up and describe some early experiences with their caregivers as negative, but they also note other experiences that were not negative and that could be considered loving. For example, Scott described his childhood relationship with his mom as inconsistent when asked by his therapist, who then asked for a *specific* autobiographical episode that showed how it was inconsistent. Scott said, "Hmm. I guess I will have to give you two memories." He went on to describe how much his single mom helped him study when he was failing a math class, instead of getting mad at him for having an F. However, Scott shared another episode that wasn't as positive. One night, when he was playing his Super Mario Brothers game before bed, his mother's boyfriend came into the room and yelled at him to turn it down, but Scott's hand slipped and he accidentally turned it up, which led to shouting about how he never listened. Scott recalled that his mother did not ever comfort him about this home situation or acknowledge how tough it was to have a man in the house who was mean to Scott a lot.

In this scenario, we can clearly see a little boy longing for love and comfort and notice a clear demonstration of both loving and unloving experiences. Despite how painful this experience was (and perhaps still is), Scott was able to share it in a relatively calm and convincing manner. This is very difficult. Researchers have referred to people who have overcome these types of harsh childhood experiences and are able to discuss them in a contained and cogent way in adulthood as an *earned secure* Networker.

I sometimes think of this as a "But God" style or substyle of the Networker. The odds were stacked against this person from their early days, *but God* intervened and brought another loving person into their life to show them responsive contingent care when their primary caregiver was not able to. The existence of the earned secure style breathes hope into the insecure heart. Earned secure adults have been shown to parent their children in ways that are just as effective as those with the Networker's style, despite tending to deal with higher levels of depressive symptoms. They're also involved in high-quality romantic relationships. Their relationships tend to be just as valuable and fulfilling to them as the prototypical secure Networker. They have greater attunement and emotional presence than the Firefighter, Investigator, and Security Guard.[2]

Kintsugi is a beautiful Japanese art form. Kintsugi is translated "golden repair" or "golden joinery." When a piece of pottery is broken, it isn't discarded or thrown away. The pottery is mended, but it isn't mended with the same contents used to create it. It's mended using lacquer that's been mixed with powdered gold. The cracks are then considered part of the history of the object.

The earned secure Networker has scars filled with golden lacquer. Like the high-functioning Firefighter, Investigator, or Security Guard, the earned secure Networker may have walked through a range of painful experiences, but because they've made meaning of their experiences, they've been able to incorporate them into part of their story.

Increasing Security: Developing a High-Functioning Relationship Style

You can optimize your relationship style by using a variety of interventions to become more secure. Despite a lack of loving experiences as a child, you can have high-quality, loving relationships in adulthood.

How does this happen? Many ways—but the suggestion to keep a journal (in your pocket or purse if possible) you've seen in these pages is quite helpful. This is a frequent recommendation from counselors, psychologists, and relationship coaches (and is also a recommendation in apps that help clients cope with ADHD) because it is a simple practice with a big impact. Keep your journal with you and make a note when you notice any feelings of discomfort in relationships or feelings that pop up inside and the events that correspond to them. See if you start noticing feelings bubbling up into awareness more often after starting this process. Remember, to have a healthy relationship, you have to have intimacy with another person, and this requires being able to share parts of yourself so they can truly know you. Try to write down your feelings, behaviors, and relationship movement (toward, away, or entangled). For example, consider this client's excerpt:

Situation: Colleague suggested taking my idea out of the marketing pitch.

Thoughts: Why is she rejecting my idea? I like her but wish she would say something positive about my ideas. I wonder if she hates all of them and dislikes my work. I wonder if she dislikes me.

Feelings: Sad, tense, anxious.

Behavior: Had a drink to reduce tension, despite trying to quit.

Practice journaling like this—particularly noting your thoughts and feelings—and eventually this practice will increase awareness and emotional intelligence, which will benefit you on your quest toward a higher-functioning style.

The journey to security—from the Firefighter's survivor style to less anxiety and avoidance—can ultimately lead to a high-functioning Firefighter style. The high-functioning Firefighter is aware of their triggers and is aware of when they use distancing strategies (like the Security Guard) or more hyperactivating strategies (like the Investigator) and is at work on their struggles. Over time, through counseling, reflection, and personal development, this person may even change styles altogether. These practices could lead to the movement from the Security Guard's aloof style to the Networker's approachable and intimate style or from the Investigator's anxious worrisome style to the Networker's easy-breezy style. This is called earning security.

There's still more to learn about the journey, which isn't a straight linear path but a long and winding road. It's important to remember that the circuitous route itself can be seen as a gift with many lessons awaiting the sojourner around each bend. However, there are some clear strategies and pathways.

Three common landmarks on nearly all paths to security include the following:

- Making sense of early difficult experiences with caregivers to be able to communicate about them coherently without minimizing their impact.
- Revising relationship blueprints (internal working models).
- Having high-quality responsive relationships. Good relationships are therapeutic on their own and can help on the journey of becoming. Some attachment experts have called these special healing relationships "emotionally corrective experiences."[3] Some depression experts, such as CBASP pioneer Dr. Jim McCullough, have called the strategies that therapists use to facilitate these experiences interventions, like "disciplined personal involvement." My pastor friends call them "healing relationships in the body of Christ."

Why Pursue a More Secure Relationship Style?

The more secure a person's relationship style is, the more it buffers the toxic effect that self-doubt has on their self-esteem. For example, if Johnny is a Networker and a perfectionist, he'll be inclined to criticize himself if he didn't do as well as he'd like on a test. This may be due to distorted thoughts that prompt him to exaggerate his personal responsibility and diminish his self-efficacy.

However, if Johnny has Networker bonds with his classmates, they'll give him support and feedback to help him correct these cognitive distortions (faulty thoughts). This support from his peer network will help decrease the impact of his negative thoughts and boost his self-esteem.

On the other hand, if Johnny has the Security Guard or Firefighter style, he'll be less inclined to open up to friends to make sense of this stressful situation. He won't have the same opportunity to receive feedback to reduce his distress, so his self-esteem may take an unnecessary blow based on his performance.

Let's take a look at how we might modify certain relational terrain for security with each relationship style.

The Security Guard's Journey toward Security

The Security Guard may have the shortest but most uncomfortable journey toward security and is least likely to decide to take it on their own. Why? The other three styles are inclined to move toward relationships and relational healing, while the Security Guard does not. The Security Guard has had lots of experiences with rejection during childhood whether subtle or direct. A pushing away became the predominant feature in their childhood relationships, which ultimately produced premature independence. Thus, during adulthood, they have learned what it's like to be rebuffed in relationship; now they're the one throwing up the relational roadblocks. They're the one saying, "Let's both drive and meet there" or "We don't need to do everything together." Their primary stance becomes a valuing of independence over relationship and pushing prospective partners away.

As an adult Security Guard, you may continue to remain aloof, feeling uncomfortable when people approach your boundaries. Maybe you retain a safe distance, since that helped you get your needs met as a child. You notice that when conversation partners take a step closer at a party, you quietly take a step back to maintain some distance. Try to stop yourself. Instead, lean into the discomfort.

Sure, dismissing your feelings and other people helped you keep from alienating your caregivers further as a child. You've become fiercely independent and that is the way you like it. But how does this serve you today? What if there could be a better way?

Expressing vulnerable emotions or connecting to a partner's vulnerable emotions can *seem* like foreign terrain for the Security Guard, better left untread.

But today is a new day. Let's look at some ideas for the Security Guard to decrease avoidance:

- Notice that if you remain on the path of least resistance, pursuing other interests and turning away from love and connection, you are likely to end up single long-term. If you want to have a satisfying relationship, learn to lean into the discomfort.
- Challenge yourself to go to therapy and find a psychologist or counselor who can help you turn toward connection during times of distress. Find someone who can help you increase your comfort with expressing emotions. Remember a counselor or psychologist is supposed to help you process through emotions.
- Don't be afraid of the hard questions. After expressing your feelings in a journal, try expressing them to a life coach or to a therapist in a safe environment where you can receive validation.
- Use a feeling wheel to build your repertoire of feeling words and see your emotional vocabulary grow and identify the primary feeling underneath the feeling. If you ask yourself, "How am I feeling?" and your answer is "Fine," ask yourself, "What is underneath the fine?" Or, as Dr. John Kuhnley likes to say about his work with clients, "Never stop at fine."

- Catch yourself idealizing to create distance. If you find yourself falling in love with the idea of who a person is on the outside rather than who they are on the inside, ask yourself, "What does it feel like to interact with this person? When we chat, what do I feel?"
- Practice receiving support. Pay attention when your friends or dates do come through for you. Do they show up when they say they will? Do they let you know if they will be late?
- Practice self-compassion and be kind to yourself, knowing that this movement toward a more secure style is a marathon and not a sprint.

We all get comfortable with what we're used to, even if it's painful. For example, if you had parents who were critical and rejecting, you probably have a loud internal critic and you find yourself drawn to people who are more sarcastic and critical, creating the same experiences you had in childhood. This is natural, but it may keep you feeling lonely. Instead, try to expose yourself to folks who give you warm and fuzzy messages. It could be a pastor who reminds you how much God loves you, a therapist who reminds you to practice kind self-talk, a massage therapist who reminds you to take Epsom salt baths and drink lots of water, or a restaurant server who calls you all sorts of terms of endearment. Try to accept these kind messages and journal about your thoughts, feelings, and responses. As you lean into the discomfort and practice journaling, your self-compassion will grow and then you can extend this compassion to relationship partners.

Now that you have awareness of these items, this opens the door to metacognitive monitoring—the capacity to think about your thinking. Self-awareness in and of itself is a secure tendency. The more you practice this process of reflection, monitoring, leaning into the discomfort, and turning toward connections, the shorter the journey will be to a more secure relationship style.

The Investigator's Journey toward Security

The Investigator has gathered hurts and worries and hauls the luggage around until it gets so heavy, they collapse under the weight. Their imagination runs away with them when they don't hear from their partner for a while, and they consider all the things that could be luring them away. They wonder whether their partner would be calling and spending time with them if they were more attractive, intelligent, charismatic, charming, organized, or fun.

If there were an Olympic medal for jumping to conclusions, the Investigator would take the gold. If fretting were a pro sport, they'd be at the top of their game. And as we know, these skills originated in childhood.

The Investigator experienced a lack of an important ingredient for trust and safety—*consistency*. Their experiences felt quite unloving and were hard to make sense of. But the Investigator put on their investigative cap, picked up their magnifying glass, and tried to figure things out, often getting stuck on preoccupation. Investigators set aside their needs in order to please their important relationship figures until their needs became so intense that their emotions came out like a volcanic eruption. (Without intentional work, this may still happen in their adult romantic relationships.)

Inevitably, bitterness, anger, and preoccupation emerged. Fearfulness also manifested, as there may have been a fear or anxiety about displeasing the caregiver and thus never being worthy of care.

In adulthood, the Investigator finds themselves very in tune with what others are feeling. They may even be high in "advanced empathy," which involves picking up on someone else's feelings even before they're aware of what they feel. The Investigator is at risk for over-empathizing with their partners. They have to learn to care without carrying the weight of others' struggles on their shoulders. It can be a challenge for the Investigator to establish boundaries and comfortably know where their responsibilities for their loved ones end. Part of the Investigator's journey to higher functioning involves avoiding carrying false guilt.

Investigators have to learn to care without carrying the weight of others' struggles on their shoulders.

Leaving Chaos Behind and Moving Ahead in Romantic Relationships

Unfortunately, we cannot go back for a do-over. Remaining preoccupied with past unmet needs won't help the Investigator be who they're meant to be relationally. Instead, the Investigator can acknowledge that they did not get the consistent support they needed, extend self-compassion, and focus on what is working now. The Investigator's keen attunement, sensitivity, awareness, preoccupation, and hypervigilance with the emotions and needs of others served them well during childhood. But these practices must be refocused in adulthood.

When the Investigator encounters prospective romantic partners who are high-functioning Security Guards or Networkers, they will need to change their approach. Preoccupation has long been central to the Investigator's state of mind, but it will be necessary to set down the magnifying glass and find what's good about their prospective partner while still remaining attuned to any red flags. It can help for an Investigator to work with a counselor or have accountability with a trusted friend or a relationship coach so that they can reality-check their narratives in their relationship story. When an Investigator starts experiencing feelings of love and infatuation, their emotional intuition immediately takes a back seat to pleasing their partner.

The Investigator may do well to date multiple partners, date in groups, or date more casually before committing to one partner as preoccupation may make it challenging for them to disengage from partners that trigger their relationship system.

If you're an Investigator, you may tend to ruminate on wrongs when people have hurt you, but it is important to let go of the bitterness, anger, resentment, and fear that's accumulated over the years. Revising the rules, leaning into the idea that you are worthy of love, and embracing new relationship beliefs takes constant metacognitive monitoring and commitment to revisions.

Deconstructing the "Not Good Enough" Myth

The Investigator tends to be high in relationship anxiety and worry, but there are strategies to address this. Journaling and naming feelings can help, as well as remembering that their feelings matter.

And as a Christ follower, it's important to remember *spiritual* truths: You are good enough. The Son of God believes this so much that He was willing to give His life for your ransom. He paid the price for your sins so you could spend eternity with Him. God loves you so sacrificially that He was willing to give His life to die for you.

You are created in the image of Almighty God, the Creator of the universe. God loves you so much that He's adopted you into His family and called you His child. You are a son or daughter of the King of Kings and Lord of Lords. The Lord promises that if your caregivers forsake you, He will care for you, take you up, and hold you close. You are good enough.

Strategies for Increasing Security

Self-compassion is another valuable and essential tool in the toolbox for building a secure foundation. There is a biblical basis for this. The Bible commands: "Therefore, as God's people, holy and dearly loved, clothe yourselves with compassion, kindness, humility, gentleness and patience" (Col. 3:12). The Scriptures encourage us not only to practice compassion but to *clothe* ourselves with it. Thus, compassion is something we should "put on" each day.

As we extend compassion toward ourselves, we also extend it to those around us. As we practice, we continue to extend the circle of compassion wider and wider.

Dr. Patti Hinkley, Dr. Holly Johnson, Dr. Tiberio Garza, and some of our graduate students have been working with me on some research on the impact of self-care workshops that serve to develop empathy and reduce relationship style–related anxiety. We've found that adults—particularly Investigators—who tend to be high in anxiety about relationships also tend to worry whether their partners really love them. They fear losing their partner's love and tend to worry that they don't measure up when comparing themselves to others.[4]

When these same workshop participants completed exercises designed to increase their mindfulness and self-compassion, we found something very interesting. Self-compassion could predict up to a 26 percent *decrease* in relationship style anxiety and shift toward a more secure style of relating. I recently created a video tutorial guide, which you can view on YouTube, to practice a short self-compassion exercise at https://www.youtube .com/watch?v=MxniNM_YV3c.

The Firefighter's Journey toward Security

Owning our stories—especially our stories of struggle—is not easy. The Firefighter has had more than their fair share of hardships and faces the longest and most circuitous route to earned security. The Firefighter may arrive marred by sweat and blood. Like the little girl named Much Afraid in the allegorical novel

Hinds' Feet on High Places, the Firefighter may feel ill-equipped for the long, winding, and often uphill journey. Much Afraid felt this way when the Shepherd invited her to journey to the high places.

A daughter of the fearing clan, she dwelled in the Valley of Humiliation. She had one crippled leg, and her face was disfigured. When she reflected upon her bodily limitations, she felt unworthy to enter into the high places, and as she contemplated the journey, her confidence waned. So, what was Much Afraid to do? The answer was clear: she had to do what every successful person of faith before her had done—lean into the discomfort and place her trust in the good Shepherd. He understood her concerns and listened to her fears with compassion. The Shepherd assured her that she could call on Him for help and that He would provide her companions for the journey.[5]

Perhaps you resonate with the symbolism in Much Afraid's journey of transformation. You, too, can experience the comforting, steadying words of the Great Shepherd. If you resonate with the Firefighter's style, please add *Hinds' Feet on High Places* to your book list. It's one I have read time and time again, gaining something new each time. This may help you feel a sense of God's presence, carrying you as a shepherd carries a lamb, as you embark on your own journey of becoming.

The Firefighter, too, survived scary experiences, difficult family situations, perceived personal limitations, and many more roadblocks to relationship security. Remarkably, in counseling we hear many accounts of Firefighters experiencing healing relationships that involve supportive others who help them revise their beliefs about whether they're worthy of love and whether others can show them love reliably. The high-functioning Firefighter differs from the low-functioning Firefighter in enhanced self-awareness, an effort to nurture metacognition, efforts at healing and revising relationship blueprints (whether through counseling, journaling, EMDR therapy, or a combination of these practices), and intentional decision-making about how or if to interact with loved ones who may have a detrimental effect on personal well-being.

It is also important to find a healing community. Making supportive friends in adulthood can be hard; some people find these relationships emerge out of church small groups and group therapy or perhaps through AA, NA, or other self-help groups. Therapeutic relationships with a counselor are inherently healing and serve an important role in the journey of becoming. I recommend counseling for support in pursuing a high-functioning relationship style. Even my training to become a therapist required me to pursue my own counseling with a minimum of three sessions. Since the Firefighter deals with both the challenges of the Investigator and the Security Guard, they can benefit from all of the aforementioned strategies—as well as those that follow.

Priming Security

One strategy the Firefighter can use on the journey to security is *priming*. Once, when I was at an attachment conference in New York City, an attachment researcher, Dr. Jude Cassidy, asked a few powerful questions that can help usher in a secure state of mind.

She asked the audience, "How do you feel when you feel secure?"

People shouted out words like *relaxed, calm, good*.

Do what you would do if you felt secure.

Then Dr. Cassidy asked an even more revealing question: "How do you behave when you feel secure?"

One-word responses emerged from the crowd: *kind, considerate, helpful*.

Then she said, "Do what you would do if you felt secure." She shared that she keeps these words on signs on her fridge and in her office.

The Mister Rogers Effect: Ten-Second Transformation

Though Mister Rogers died nearly twenty years ago, his impact can still be felt. For example, every time there's a public tragedy, his well-known words, "look for the helpers," circulate again. His therapeutic impact was uncanny. Several accounts were reported of children with seizure disorders who ceased from seizing when listening to his voice. After he spoke to a suicidal child, that child *never* thought or talked about suicide again.

How did Mister Rogers have such a therapeutic effect on so many people around him? Each time he spoke—whether at an awards ceremony or a high school graduation—he asked a powerfully positive question.

He'd acknowledge that many people in our lives help us get where we are today, and then he'd encourage his listeners to take time to think about those people who loved them into being *who they were*. He'd remind them that those people may be nearby, they may be far away, or they may even be in heaven.

He'd finish by inviting listeners to take ten seconds to think about those who loved the good that grows within them. And he'd keep the time.

It was a powerful pause.

This exercise can be powerful for you today too. If you can combine this activity with imagining that loved one giving you a hug or a pat on the back, you'll eventually be able to usher in thoughts of security and feelings of being loved and at peace. If you pair this imagining with a physical gesture, such as giving yourself a butterfly hug or snapping your fingers, eventually you will find that the hugging or snapping alone may provoke those secure feelings due to the power of positive association.

Accountability Partners

I recommend finding a trusted friend that you feel safe with in your unguarded moments to serve as an accountability partner. Blame keeps people stuck, so finding a cushion of care can be very helpful in the healing journey. The narrative of the Networker and the earned secure Networker is balanced and free of self-blame and blaming others. An accountability partner may be a prayer partner, a sponsor through a self-help organization, a friend who is also pursuing growth and healing, or someone who has earned your trust. Unfortunately, there are no guarantees, but part of the journey toward security involves learning that love is worth the risk.

Safe Spaces

Students often ask if it's possible to have two different relationship styles or to have different relationship styles in different relationships. Based on relationship style–testing research, we tend to develop a primary style and apply the relationship blueprints in many different relationships. That is, we develop a set of beliefs about whether we're worthy of love and whether others are able to show love. Then we modify those relationship blueprints based on experiences, and these guide our behaviors in relationships.

Researchers call these *working models* since we can revise them. If you never had positive experiences with caregivers, teachers, or mentors, you're not alone. Mister Rogers became a substitute attachment/relationship figure for many young people who didn't have any adults around to go to. Through his programming, he did many of the things a loving caregiver would do, which offered young viewers a safe haven. As we discussed earlier, it can be healing to meditate on the expressions of care Mister Rogers provided to nurture and develop your internal, compassionate caregiver.

When early experiences are difficult or traumatic, we develop hypervigilance. Though not helpful in every situation, hypervigilance is a coping skill necessary for survival. Learning to shift our nervous system from a sympathetic state of high arousal (fight, flight, freeze, or fawn) to a parasympathetic state of calm (relax, rest, and digest) is no easy feat. We can get comfortable feeling uncomfortable—until we slowly learn to use tools and find safe spaces to calm us.

Faith as a Safe Haven

The apostle Peter was encouraged to step out of the safety of his boat onto the water to approach his Lord in the midst of a storm. Only when he took his eyes off his safe haven, Jesus, did he start to sink (see Matt. 14).

The doubts about God's goodness emerge explicitly in Peter's perception. Jesus sees this and challenges Peter to revise these thoughts. Like Peter, we can all be plagued by doubt of the goodness of God. We can all face the question about our faith in those telling moments of distress. But we do not have to face our religious doubt alone. Jesus reaches out to us and invites us to pursue the journey to the high places with Him—where we know we're worthy of love. He paid the ultimate price for us even while we were still sinners. God's able to love us, even though it often may not come in the way we hope or expect.

Right now, we see only a dim reflection of who we are and who God is. But the Bible says one day we'll see in full. Our human relationships are limited by our imperfect state of being. Each relationship we have, no matter how important, will arrive at its inevitable end, and we will have to say our final goodbyes—perhaps in death, in divorce, or growing apart emotionally. Even thoughts of ending can activate our relationship system and expose our doubts about our worthiness of love and the dependability of others.

Jesus offers the possibility of a relationship without end. Here enters the concept of God attachment. We can relate to God as an attachment or relationship figure. God has many names throughout the Bible: Yahweh, Jehovah Jireh, Emmanuel, and many more. Jesus could've picked any one of those names, but He specifically commanded us to pray in such a way that we address God as "our Father."

The lyrics to "Out of Hiding (Father's Song)" by Steffany Gretzinger and Amanda Cook describe the journey of the Firefighter. The song is a reminder that God invites us to stop hiding our feelings and a reminder of this important truth: we can cast our cares on the Lord; we are safe with Him. We're encouraged to throw our cares away and make a run for the Father.

Consider this line from the song: "What hindered love will only become part of the story."[6] Challenging times can become integrated into the greater narrative of our lives, and we can make sense of them in light of the Father's love for us. From our safe haven, we know that God can redeem our most painful experiences. The painful experiences have to be integrated into our story in a meaningful way, which is no easy feat. Journaling, counseling, prayer, meditation, and healing relationships are part of the journey.

Summary: Putting the Pieces Together

Relationship styles influence everything we do and can play a primary role in whether we experience passionate, loving relationships; disconnected and dull relationships; or conflicted and unfulfilling relationships. If you want to know the likely outcome of a relationship, one great way to predict it is by looking at a person's relationship style. And by identifying your own primary style, you are making serious headway on your journey toward optimization. A hope-building reminder is that it is not your experiences that influence your relationship style the most but how you think of and make sense of them. You can learn which relationship style you have by taking the quiz in chapter 3. There's also a more comprehensive assessment online. Visit DrAnitaKuhnley.com for more information.

The good news is whatever relationship style you have right now, you can improve it and become more secure. You can work to secure your heart, mind, and relationships through the strategies we have discussed in this book. And you can find safe havens that work for you, which will help you reengage with the world.

Recapping Emotion Regulation

When it comes to emotion regulation, it is most helpful to discuss it from the perspective of relationship styles and the relationship behavioral system we highlighted earlier.

When we have support in organizing our feelings from a loved one who serves as the safe haven in our stormy sea, we can be calmed easily. From this calm place of support (known as our secure base), we can launch out to engage with the world around us and serve others freely and purposefully. Even the Savior of the world, when He stood up to serve humanity, remembered His relationship security. "Jesus knew that the Father had put all things under his power, and that he had come from God and was returning to God; so he got up from the meal, took off his outer clothing, and wrapped a towel around his waist" (John 13:3–4).

Jesus knew that He had come from His safe haven, God, and that He was returning back to His secure base at the right hand of the Father. So He was able to rise to the top side of the Circle of Security with confidence and serve humanity humbly. Then, on the bottom side of the circle, in His darkest hours, He cried out to His Father before He returned to home base. He did all of this out of love for us.

Relationship Styles and Emotion Regulation

Firefighter	Investigator	Security Guard	Networker
No clear strategy; wants to move toward a loved one but may experience the loved one blaming them or making things worse; may alternate randomly between approach and avoid	Starts to move toward loved ones but is overwhelmed or flooded with emotions so may get tangled up in expressing feelings appropriately	Moves away from loved ones to process emotions independently	Moves toward loved ones for help organizing and processing emotions
Feels stuck and overwhelmed by emotions; may randomly alternate between the other responses in a chaotic way	May exaggerate emotions or get flooded by them	Minimizes the experience and expression of emotions	Is comfortable expressing a range of emotions to partners and loved ones
Tends to be flooded by emotions and gets overwhelmed; feels stuck not knowing where to turn or how to cope with them; may engage in tension-reduction behaviors, like addictions	May experience hyperactivation of emotion; may try to please partner and stuff feelings of anger or disappointment until they are overwhelming and then erupt	Avoids disclosing feelings and turns away from emotions and emotion-related content; seeks to deactivate emotions	Is able to trust and disclose vulnerable emotions and quickly experiences soothing and comfort
No clear organization of emotions in relationships	May get tangled up in emotional intimacy, letting feelings build up until they are overwhelming	Low emotional intimacy; difficult and uncomfortable being emotionally present	High emotional intimacy

The Path toward Security

Now that you have some tools and enhanced awareness to help you on the journey of optimizing your style, you know how to rewrite your story without allowing anxiety and avoidance to overwhelm the narrative. It may be a nonlinear narrative for now, but navigating home to a secure relationship will be time well spent.

Though our time together in this book is coming to a close, remember that you have a God who journeys with you, and He has not brought you this far in the journey of healing in your relationship style to leave you. He will illuminate everything and see the journey through to completion!

We are never alone; we have a safe haven and secure base in Jesus. He taught us what true love is through His sacrificial love on the cross, and He invites us to approach connection and relationship by coming to Him just as we are.

Remember, you can prime security by thinking of a secure relationship from your past. For example, I often think of my Mims, who loved to pray the Aaronic blessing over her family, and I would like to pray this blessing over you, dear reader, as you continue your journey:

> The LORD bless you
>   and keep you,
> the LORD make His face shine on you
>   and be gracious to you;
> the LORD turn his face toward you
>   and give you peace.
>
> Numbers 6:24–26

GLOSSARY

anterior cingulate gyrus: The part of the human brain involved with emotions, learning, and memory; because of this, it is influential in linking behavior to outcome. In keeping with Dr. Daniel Amen's definition, we have called it the brain's gearshift.

avoidant style: Another name for the Security Guard. This relationship style is characterized by the tendency to move away from connection and keep others at arm's length. *See also* dismissing style.

Circle of Security: An image that describes two behavioral systems we learn in childhood to help us manage stress and interact with the world: (1) how to explore the world (launch from a secure base), and (2) what we do when threatened by the world (retreat to our safe haven).

Our secure base is represented on the left side: when we feel secure, we launch from there to the top of the circle; on the opposite (right) side, we encounter threats and plummet to the bottom of the circle where we are in need of help organizing our feelings and welcomed home. This Circle of Security has been popularized by Dr. Bob Marvin's work.

dialectical behavioral therapy (DBT): Training developed by Marsha Linehan that involves a set of skills to help with emotion regulation. DBT includes many interventions, some of which help you identify triggers that lead to feelings of being emotionally overwhelmed and provide coping mechanisms to reduce them.

dismissing style: The Security Guard. Characterized by a tendency to minimize wanting, needing, and valuing in relationships, a preference for independence, and a movement away from connection. *See also* avoidant style.

dismissing tendencies: Tendencies to deactivate emotion and move away from relationship.

earned secure: Describes people who have overcome harsh childhood experiences, are able to discuss their experiences in a contained and cogent way in adulthood, and can demonstrate secure tendencies. Also called the "But God" style.

emotional intelligence: The ability to be aware of your emotions and to understand and manage them. Emotional intelligence has been conceptualized as a collection of fifteen different traits (e.g., optimism, stress management, low impulsivity), and also as a set of key abilities, such as the ability to use emotional information to facilitate thought, understand emotion, and regulate emotions.

fearful avoidant style: The Firefighter. Also known as "cannot classify." Characterized by high anxiety about relationship partners and high avoidance with regard to intimacy and closeness in relationships. This is a disorganized response that randomly fluctuates between strategies the other styles use in a more organized fashion.

feeling wheel (or feeling faces): Similar to a color wheel, a feeling wheel, often used in therapy, illustrates human feelings/emotions on a pie chart with core emotions in the center, and other feeling words that correspond to them in the outer circles.

fight, flight, freeze, or fawn: Fight (engage in conflict), flight (exit the situation right away), freeze (don't move), or fawn (engage in people-pleasing behaviors to avoid conflict).

high-functioning: With respect to relationship styles, a person who seeks to be self-aware, identifies triggers, actively seeks to resolve dissonance between their thoughts and feelings, and seeks to move toward emotions and relationships (at times even in the face of discomfort).

love languages: A framework for understanding how we give and receive love as made popular in *The 5 Love Languages* by Dr. Gary Chapman. The five languages are words of affirmation, quality time, receiving gifts, acts of service, and physical touch.

low-functioning: With respect to relationship styles, a person who has high levels of avoidance and/or anxiety and is not aware of their triggers; these issues interfere with their functioning and capacity to have satisfying relationships.

metacognitive monitoring: Thinking about your thinking; self-awareness.

optimized/optimizing: Making the most of your emotional profile through specific practices, such as therapy, meditation, and developing healthy relationships; seeking to increase self-awareness, decrease anxiety, decrease avoidance, and increase comfort with closeness; includes moving toward growth in emotional intelligence and the capacity to connect.

organized response: A strategy one uses for dealing with relationships that has a consistent plan that will be the same every time.

parasympathetic nervous system: A network of nerves that helps us relax and experience a state of comfort (think, rest, and digest), which is associated with top-down thinking.

Can be thought of as the brain's braking system that helps slow us down. (Contrast **sympathetic nervous system.**)

prefrontal cortex (PFC): The front part of the human brain that organizes thoughts and actions to follow predetermined goals. It moderates planning, decision-making, and social behavior.

preoccupied style: The Investigator. Also called entangled style. *See also* preoccupied tendencies.

preoccupied tendencies: The tendency to get preoccupied with angry or fearful thoughts and/or feelings, to circle in conversation, to violate relevance through conversational detours, and to get entangled in relationships, including tendencies to blame, identify inconsistencies, and mistrust a relationship partner.

projection: A defense mechanism in which you project your feelings onto your partner (e.g., you are angry, so you accuse your partner of being angry).

QTIP: An acronym for Quit Taking It Personally. It helps us remember that relationship rules are not personal.

relationship blueprint: An internal working model that explains how we think about relationships with other humans. It consists of the answers to two questions: (1) Am I worthy of love? (2) Can others be counted on to love me?

relationship styles: Another term for the more scientific "attachment styles."

safe haven: *See* Circle of Security.

secure autonomous style: The Networker. Characterized by low anxiety, low avoidance, a movement toward connection, comfort with sharing emotion, comfort with both giving and receiving support, and a tendency to highly value relationships.

secure base: *See* Circle of Security.

secure/insecure: Secure refers to the organized relationship style that is the most adaptive (what we have called the Networker's style), characterized by movement toward connection, comfort with closeness, low anxiety, low avoidance, comfort with emotional discussion, and a willingness to share feelings with partners.

Insecure styles include two organized styles, preoccupied (Investigator) and dismissing (Security Guard), and one disorganized style (Firefighter). These styles tend to be characterized by less comfort with closeness and varying combinations of higher levels of anxiety and/or avoidance.

soft start-up: Starting a discussion with a partner using a soft and gentle tone. This is much more effective than a harsh start-up and is brought to us courtesy of Dr. John Gottman's research. Soft start-up has been shown to predict positive outcomes in conflict and is associated with more relationship longevity than a harsh start-up.

sympathetic nervous system: Associated with bottom-up thinking and fight, flight, freeze, and fawn behavior, due to a perceived threat and hyperarousal of the nervous system. Can be conceptualized as the brain's gas pedal that helps rev us up. (Contrast **parasympathetic nervous system.**)

ACKNOWLEDGMENTS

The science behind *The Four Relationship Styles* comes from attachment theory, which is sometimes affectionately called the scientific study of love. On our journey of becoming, we are blessed to encounter others who teach us what love is (and perhaps those who teach us what it isn't). Some of my earliest teachers in this regard include my mother and my grandmothers. My grandma Jean introduced me to Love Himself, the Lord Jesus Christ, who has led me on a journey of becoming since long before I knew who He was. Grandma Jean died when I was eight years old and left me with a children's book about the birth of Christ, which she inscribed with the words, "Anita, my Darling granddaughter, learn well about Jesus." That has been the chief mission of my life.

I am thankful for our heavenly Father who gets the glory for any work I am involved with. He is my source of inspiration, my sustainer of energy and strength, and my rock. He is the only One who can bring true healing and restoration to the relationship system, and I am thankful that He leads all of us on our journey of becoming and invites us into relationship with Him as our Father and the Lover of our souls.

I am thankful for my Mims who believed in me, encouraged me, supported me, and helped me feel God's presence throughout some of the most difficult times of my life. Her photo stays on my desk, and her words and loving spirit continue to nourish my soul.

I am also thankful for my parents. Especially my mother, who, in the wake of my grandmother Jean's death, when I was despondent and tuned out at school, took the extra time and with great patience taught me how to read. I owe her a debt of gratitude. I am thankful for all of my family members, especially my siblings, for the opportunity to be a part of your journey. Paul, thank you for always letting me use your story in my classes and in my writing. I am also especially thankful for my cousin Roly, who believes in me and encourages me and is generous with his pep talks; my cousin Maria, who is quick to pray with me and offer support and encouragement; and my cousins Dan and Charles Mike, whose writing feedback is always helpful and constructive.

Dr. John Kuhnley, thank you for your insights, encouragement, and support along the long journey of developing this manuscript and the corresponding materials. Your love, encouragement, intellectual camaraderie, and belief in me make all the difference. I could not have done this without you.

Also, special thanks to Dr. Justin Silvey and Dr. Lisa Compton for your partnerships in sharing our research on attachment, trauma, and other important topics.

To Jamie Chavez, I owe you a debt of gratitude I cannot repay. Your generosity of time and mental bandwidth is inspiring. Your editing prowess, eye for detail, and strength at refining content has exponentially increased the quality of this manuscript, and I am so thankful to have journeyed with you on this book and *The Mister Rogers Effect*. Thank you for believing in me and having safe eyes to share the first reading of this manuscript with. You are thorough, effective, and have an excellent sense of humor—a stellar combination.

I thank Brian Vos at Baker Books who has a passion for producing pieces that help people to live their best lives. Thank you for believing in the value and importance of this work and desiring to help see it through to completion. Without your helpful spirit, honest feedback, and belief, this project would not be possible.

Many thanks to Emily Culver for your Chicago Style consultations and assistance in gathering all the research citations and endnotes to ensure everything is properly cited—your contributions are much appreciated! I am thankful for your attention to detail.

I would also like to thank Robin Turici, whose editing skills were essential in the development of this manuscript. Robin, you are kind, honest, and helpful—such an elegant combination. Thank you for going the extra mile and seeking to share your insights into how to ensure the text is one readers can enjoy reading. Your patience, time, and energy have been such a blessing. I am thankful to be able to work together once again!

Amy Nemecek, thank you for ensuring that all source citations have been correctly formatted according to the *Chicago Manual of Style*. Your attention to detail is noteworthy.

Thanks to my agent, Jim Hart, for starting me on this trajectory with my previous book *The Mister Rogers Effect*, for championing my work, and for securing it in good hands with Baker Books not once but twice! I pray your retirement is blessed; you will be missed.

Much gratitude and appreciation to my colleagues. Thank you, Dr. Laurel Shaler, for your prayer and encouragement along the way. To Dr. Lisa Compton, thank you for being my consulting counterpart, for sharing on topics related to trauma and attachment, for speaking at conferences with me across the United States, and for showing grace while much of my time went to this manuscript. We are better together! Thank you, Dr. Patti Hinkley and Dr. Justin Silvey, for mentoring our research team and working with me on countless research projects throughout the years. To Dr. Holly Johnson and Dr. Tiberio Garza, thank you for your partnership on research projects and your support and understanding of my work on this text. You are both a tremendous blessing and inspiration. To Dr. Kim Penberthy and Dr. Dorothy Kalyanapu, thank you for your feedback, support, and insights. Hannah Hearin, thank you for your encouragement and support.

I remain deeply affected by my mentors, Dr. George Jefferson and Dr. Gary Sibcy, to whom I owe a debt I cannot repay. Dr. Gary Sibcy, thank you for serving as my mentor, research partner, coauthor, and our best man. I appreciate your partnership on research, in coauthoring several books and articles, and in copresenting at conferences. Each discovery we have made has increased my thirst to learn more; thank you for awakening this passion for the study of attachment and emotional intelligence in me. Your understanding of the complexities of the ever-changing field of attachment and generosity of spirit is appreciated. Dr. George Jefferson, my clinical supervisor, professor, mentor, and spiritual shepherd, has been one of the most influential people in my professional life. Dr. J, thank you for being "He who blessed with Love Himself" and for always pointing me to the Father through your mentoring and teachings. I am eternally grateful for you.

Much gratitude goes to Dr. Eric Scalise, not only for writing the foreword for this book but also for taking the time to advise me and handing me the book that began my journey all those years ago. You have been a source of inspiration, and the book you handed me so many years ago was the beginning of my lifelong journey to research, study, and understand attachment. Thank you for being a source of support and encouragement during our Regent days and beyond.

Many thanks to Amy Beldon for journeying alongside me through much clinical work and supervision. You have had a great impact and influence on my career and my early days of writing for clinical purposes. Thank you for believing in me and my work.

Special thanks to those in the field who have come before us and on whose shoulders we stand, especially Dr. John Bowlby who devoted his life to the study of attachment; Mary Ainsworth, his faithful research partner; and Bob Marvin, Mary Main, and their professional offspring who have also served as my teachers and mentors in direct and indirect ways. I am thankful for others who have contributed to the research in important ways. There are too many to mention, but you know who you are. Thank you for your contributions.

Thanks to my ballroom dance teachers, Misha Vlasov and Marina Vlasov, who teach me much about dance and life, giving me a great outlet to celebrate at each stage of the writing and editing process! Your friendship and partnership bring me great joy. I appreciate your inspiration and support. Misha and Marina, thank you for your creativity in choreographing a special routine to demonstrate each of the four relationship styles. Your creativity and body awareness are a gift, and co-creating with you is one of my great joys.

I am thankful to Tiberio Garza, Gary Sibcy, and Chris Ostrander for helping to develop, validate, and provide expert review for the attachment assessment utilized here, as well as for your collegial and helpful spirits. Also special thanks to Kristin MacDowall for brainstorming and having discussions that have been a great catalyst for this text. Thanks to my friends and colleagues Crystal Sorrelle, Hannah Hearin, Scott Mullinix, and Chris Edwards. Thank you to my friends that were so gracious to allow your stories to be used! Special thanks goes to Jen and Jason Lowe and Dave and Donna Spangler.

I could not have completed this and other writing projects without the support of many Liberty and Regent administrators who have encouraged my writing. Thanks to Dr. William Hathaway, Dr. Kenyon Knapp, Dr. Kevin Van Wynsberg, Dr. Holly Johnson, and Dr. Stacey Lilley.

To my clients and my students, thank you for allowing me to be a part of your journey of becoming. Walking alongside you and playing a role in mentoring you is one of my greatest privileges.

Last but not least, I would like to thank my readers and all who take the time to buy, discuss, and share my work. You allow me to do what I love and to make a difference through sharing my years of study and research. Thank you for making all this possible by your interest. May the Lord bless you richly, and may your journey toward loving relationships be a rewarding and expeditious adventure. Thank you for allowing me to walk with you along the way.

NOTES

Introduction The Science of Attachment Theory

1. "We decided to use the metaphor of a journey because of the progressive nature of the road to becoming. This thought originated as we found that counselors in training are asking for specific tasks to do in counseling, but we believe that the correct approach is not a journey of 'doing' counseling but more about 'being' a counselor. The main goal of becoming is to understand that we want all to be in the process of seeking to develop healthier and more well-adjusted, adaptive, and resilient lives." Richard Justin Silvey, Gary Allen Sibcy, and Anita Knight Kuhnley, "The Journey of Becoming," in Ron Hawkins et al., *Research-Based Counseling Skills: The Art and Science of Therapeutic Empathy* (Dubuque, IA: Kendall Hunt Publishing, 2018), 39.

2. Please note, attachment theory is drawn from a wide range of scientific disciplines including psychoanalysis, ethology, cognitive psychology, and developmental psychology.

3. Jude Cassidy, "Emotion Regulation: Influences of Attachment Relationships," *Monographs for the Society of Research in Child Development* 59, no. 2/3 (1994): 228–49; Daniel J. Siegel, "Toward an Interpersonal Neurobiology of the Developing Mind: Attachment Relationships, 'Mindsight,' and Neural Integration," *Infant Mental Health Journal* 22, no. 1/2 (2001): 67–94; Marinus H. van IJzendoorn, "Adult Attachment Representations, Parental Responsiveness, and Infant Attachment: A Meta-Analysis on the Predictive Validity of the Adult Attachment Interview," *Psychological Bulletin* 117, no. 3 (1995): 387–403.

Chapter 1 What Are Relationship Styles?

1. van IJzendoorn, "Adult Attachment Representations," 395–97.

2. Eyob Ayenew, "The Effect of Adult Attachment Style on Couples Relationship Satisfaction," *The International Journal of Indian Psychology* 3, no. 2 (2006): 50. "A tendency to turn toward your partner [i.e., secure attachment]

is the basis of trust, emotional connection, passion, and a satisfying sex life." John M. Gottman and Nan Silver, *The Seven Principles for Making Marriage Work: A Practical Guide from the Country's Foremost Relationship Expert*, rev. ed. (New York: Harmony Books, 2015), 113.

3. J. Driver et al., "Couple Interaction in Happy and Unhappy Marriages: Gottman Laboratory Studies," in *Normal Family Processes: Growing Diversity and Complexity*, ed. F. Walsh (New York: Guilford Press, 2012), 57–77; J. M. Gottman, "Psychology and the Study of Marital Processes," *Annual Review of Psychology* 49 (1998): 169–97, https://doi.org/10.1146/annurev.psych.49.1.169.

4. Vered Shenaar, Uri Yatzkar, and Yosi Yaffe, "Paternal Feelings and Child's Anxiety: The Mediating Role of Father–Child Insecure Attachment and Child's Emotional Regulation," *American Journal of Men's Health* 15, no. 6 (2021): 1–13, https://journals.sagepub.com/doi/full/10.1177/15579883211067103#con1.

5. Patricia M. Crittenden, "Gifts from Mary Ainsworth and John Bowlby," *Clinical Child Psychology and Psychiatry* 22, no. 3 (2017): 436–42, https://doi.org/10.1177/1359104517716214.

6. Gottman and Silver, *Seven Principles*, 2.

7. "Adaptogens are plants and mushrooms that help your body respond to stress, anxiety, fatigue, and overall wellbeing." Cleveland Clinic Health Library, "Adaptogens," accessed March 20, 2023, https://my.clevelandclinic.org/health/drugs/22361-adaptogens.

8. Adrian Goldsworthy, "The True Story of 'Antony and Cleopatra,'" *Talk of the Nation* (NPR), September 28, 2010, https://www.npr.org/2010/09/28/130190252/the-true-story-of-antony-and-cleopatra.

9. Maud Ellmann, "The Sixth Act: Shakespeare after Joyce," in *Shakespeare and Comedy*, vol. 56 of *Shakespeare Survey: An Annual Survey of Shakespeare Studies and Production*, ed. Peter Holland (Cambridge: Cambridge University Press, 2003), 141.

10. Jennie Cohen, "5 Romances That Changed History," *History Stories*, last updated January 3, 2019, https://www.history.com/news/5-romances-that-changed-history.

11. Robbie Duchinsky and Katie White, *Trauma and Loss: Key Texts from the John Bowlby Archive* (New York: Routledge, 2020), 9.

Chapter 2 The Circle of Security

1. Anita M. Knight Kuhnley and Gary A. Sibcy II, *Redeeming Attachment: A Counselor's Guide to Facilitating Attachment to God and Earned Security* (Dubuque, IA: Kendall Hunt, 2017), 55.

2. Kuhnley and Sibcy, *Redeeming Attachment*, 55; Gary A. Sibcy and Anita M. Knight, "Emotional Intelligence and the Attachment Behavioral System," in *Social Psychology: How Other People Influence Our Thoughts and Actions*, vol. 1, ed. Randall W. Summers (Santa Barbara, CA: Greenwood, 2016), 59.

3. Sibcy and Knight, "Emotional Intelligence," 64.

4. Bob Marvin and Wanda Seagroves, presentation at Liberty University, Lynchburg, VA, April 25, 2017.

Chapter 3 Identifying Your Relationship Style

1. Ellen Fein and Sherrie Schneider, *The Rules for Online Dating: Capturing the Heart of Mr. Right in Cyberspace* (New York: Simon & Schuster, 2002).

2. Julie Schwartz Gottman, ed., *The Marriage Clinic Casebook* (New York: Norton, 2004), 96; John Gottman, *The Marriage Clinic* (New York: Norton and Company, 1999), 229.

3. Simon Sinek, *The Infinite Game* (New York: Penguin, 2019).

4. Phillip R. Shaver, Jay Belsky, and Kelly A. Brennan, "The Adult Attachment Interview and Self-Reports of Romantic Attachment: Associations across Domains and Methods," *Personal Relationships* 7, no. 1 (2000): 26, https://doi.org/10.1111/j.1475-6811.2000.tb00002.x; van IJzendoorn, "Adult Attachment Representations," 387.

5. Cindy Hazan and Phillip Shaver, "Romantic Love Conceptualized as an Attachment Process," *Journal of Personality and Social Psychology* 52, no. 3 (1987): 511–24, https://doi.org/10.1037/0022-3514.52.3.511.

6. Shaver, Belsky, and Brennan, "Adult Attachment Interview," 38; Nancy L. Collins and Stephen J. Read, "Adult Attachment, Working Models, and Relationship Quality in Dating Couples," *Journal of Personality and Social Psychology* 58, no. 4 (1990): 658, https://doi.org/10.1037/0022-3514.58.4.644.

7. Mary Dozier and R. Rogers Kobak, "Psychophysiology in Attachment Interviews: Converging Evidence for Deactivating Strategies," *Child Development* 63, no. 6 (1992): 1473, https://doi.org/10.2307/1131569.

8. Shaver, Belsky, and Brennan, "Adult Attachment Interview," 27.

9. R. Chris Fraley and Phillip R. Shaver, "Adult Attachment and the Suppression of Unwanted Thoughts," *Journal of Personality and Social Psychology* 73, no. 5 (1997): 1080–91, https://doi.org/10.1037/0022-3514.73.5.1080.

10. If you would like a more comprehensive look at your relationship style and a free report, please visit www.dranitakuhnley.com.

Chapter 4 The Firefighter

1. *As Good as It Gets*, directed by James L. Brooks (Sony Pictures, 1997).

2. Helen Z. Macdonald et al., "Longitudinal Association between Infant Disorganized Attachment and Childhood Posttraumatic Stress Symptoms," *Development and Psychopathology* 20, no. 2 (2008): 493–508.

3. Donatella Marazziti et al., "Romantic Attachment and Subtypes /Dimensions of Jealousy," *Clinical Practice and Epidemiology in Mental Health* 6 (2010): 53.

4. L. M. Mongomery, *Anne of Green Gables* (Boston: L. C. Page & Co., 1908), 18–19.

5. Jeffry A. Simpson and W. Steven Rholes, "Fearful-Avoidance, Disorganization, and Multiple Working Models: Some Directions for Future Theory and Research," *Attachment & Human Development* 4, no. 2 (2002): 225.

6. Gottman and Silver, *Seven Principles*, 51.

7. Gottman and Silver, *Seven Principles*, 50.

8. Daniel Amen, *The Brain in Love: 12 Lessons to Enhance Your Love Life* (New York: Three Rivers Press, 2009), 36.

9. Dan Siegel and Mary Hartzell, *Parenting from the Inside Out: How a Deeper Self-Understanding Can Help You Raise Children Who Thrive*, 10th anniversary ed. (New York: Penguin, 2014), chap. 7, table 9, Kindle.

10. Siegel and Hartzell, *Parenting from the Inside Out*, 173.

11. Siegel and Hartzell, *Parenting from the Inside Out*, chap. 7, table 9.

12. Siegel and Hartzell, *Parenting from the Inside Out*, chap. 7.

13. Shaver, Belsky, and Brennan, "Adult Attachment Interview," 33.

14. "How to Get Your Mind to Stop Spinning," Amen Clinics, June 18, 2019, https://www.amenclinics.com/blog/how-to-get-your-mind-to-stop-spinning/.

15. Anita Knight Kuhnley, *The Mister Rogers Effect* (Grand Rapids: Baker Books, 2020), 39.

16. Kyle Bensen, "The Magic Relationship Ratio, According to Science," The Gottman Institute, accessed July 14, 2023, https://www.gottman.com/blog/the-magic-relationship-ratio-according-science/.

17. Sonja Lyumbomirsky, *The How of Happiness: A New Approach to Getting the Life You Want* (New York: Penguin, 2007), 191.

18. John J. Gottman and Julie Schwartz Gottman, *And Baby Makes Three: The Six-Step Plan for Preserving Marital Intimacy and Rekindling Romance after Baby Arrives* (New York: Harmony Books, 2008), 6.

19. Kuhnley, *The Mister Rogers Effect*, 57–60.

20. "Father's Love Letter, HQ," YouTube video, posted by ABCredeemed, February 9, 2011, https://www.youtube.com/watch?v=zJvqmhGs1Y8.

Chapter 5 The Investigator

1. Donatella Marazziti et al., "Romantic Attachment in Patients with Mood and Anxiety Disorders," *CNS Spectrums* 12, no. 10 (2007): 751–56.

2. Mary D. Salter Ainsworth, Mary C. Blehar, Everett Waters, and Sally N. Wall, *Patterns of Attachment: A Psychological Study of the Strange Situation* (New York: Psychology Press, 2015), 122.

3. Johanna Bick, Mary Dozier, and Erica Perkins, "Convergence between Attachment Classifications and Natural Reunion Behavior among Children and Parents in a Child Care Setting," *Attachment & Human Development* 14, no. 1 (2012): 1–10.

4. Gary Sibcy, text message to author, July 20, 2022.

5. Mariëlle D. Beijersbergen, Marian J. Bakermans-Kranenburg, and Marinus H. van IJzendoorn, "The Concept of Coherence in Attachment

Interviews: Comparing Attachment Experts, Linguists, and Non-Experts," *Attachment & Human Development* 8, no. 4 (2006): 354.

6. Paul Grice, *Studies in the Way of Words* (Cambridge, MA: Harvard University Press, 1989), 26.

7. Beijersbergen, Bakermans-Kranenburg, and van IJzendoorn, "Concept of Coherence," 354.

8. Richard J. Foster, *Prayer: Finding the Heart's True Home* (San Francisco: HarperSanFrancisco, 2002), 29.

9. Gottman and Silver, *Seven Principles*, 89.

10. Antoine de Saint-Exupery, *The Little Prince* (Boston: Mariner Books, 2000), 63.

11. Anita M. Knight et al., "The Impact of Brief God Attachment Workshop Attendance on God Attachment," *Virginia Counselors Journal* 36 (2018): 48–55, https://cdn.ymaws.com/www.vcacounselors.org/resource/resmgr/journals /VCAJournalVol36.pdf; Anita M. Knight, Gary Sibcy, and Alexandra Gantt, "Intentional Empathy," in *Evidence-Based Counseling Skills: The Art and Science of Therapeutic Empathy*, ed. Ron Hawkins et al. (Dubuque, IA: Kendall Hunt, 2019), 52.

12. Anita Kuhnley, Patricia Hinkley, and Tiberio Garza, "The Impact of Self-Compassion Exercises on Attachment-Related Anxiety: A Randomized Controlled Trial" (working paper, in progress).

13. Joshua D. Foster, Michael H. Kernis, and Brian M. Goldman, "Linking Adult Attachment to Self-Esteem Stability," *Self and Identity* 6, no. 1 (2007): 64, https://doi.org/10.1080/15298860600832139.

14. David D. Burns, *Feeling Good Together: The Secret to Making Troubled Relationships Work* (New York: Broadway Books, 2008), loc. 818 of 4125, Kindle.

15. Burns, *Feeling Good Together*, 71.

16. Burns, *Feeling Good Together*, 77.

17. Burns, *Feeling Good Together*, 38.

18. John Bowlby, *Separation: Anxiety and Anger*, vol. 2 of *Attachment and Loss* (New York: Basic Books, 1973), 252.

19. John M. Gottman, *The Marriage Clinic: A Scientifically Based Marital Therapy* (New York: W. W. Norton & Company, 1999), 88.

20. Ellen Fein and Sherrie Schneider, *All the Rules: Time-tested Secrets for Capturing the Heart of Mr. Right* (New York: Grand Central Publishing, 2007), 24.

Chapter 6 The Security Guard

1. Mary Main, "Avoidance in the Service of Attachment: A Working Paper," in *Behavioral Development: The Bielefeld Interdisciplinary Project*, ed. Klaus Immelmann et al. (New York: Cambridge University Press, 1981), quoted in Gottfried Spangler and K. E. Grossman, "Biobehavioral Organization in Securely and Insecurely Attached Infants," *Child Development* 64, no. 5 (1993): 1440, https://doi.org/10.1111/j.1467-8624.1993.tb02962.x.

2. Deborah Jacobvitz, "Afterword: Reflections on Clinical Applications of the Adult Attachment Interview," in *Clinical Applications of the Adult Attachment Interview*, ed. Howard Steele and Miriam Steele (New York: Guilford Press, 2008), loc. 7234 of 7568, Kindle.

3. Howard Steele and Miriam Steele, "Ten Clinical Uses of the Adult Attachment Interview," in *Clinical Applications*, loc. 360 of 7568, Kindle.

4. Howard Steele and Miriam Steele, "Ten Clinical Uses of the Adult Attachment Interview," in *Clinical Applications*, loc. 492 of 7568.

5. Paul Grice, "Logic and Conversation," in *Speech Acts*, vol. 3 of *Syntax and Semantics*, ed. Jerry L. Morgan and Peter Cole (New York: Brill, 1975), 41–58; Mary Main, Erik Hesse, and Ruth Goldwyn, "Studying Differences in Language Usage in Recounting Attachment History, An Introduction to AAI," in *Clinical Applications*, loc. 983 of 7568.

6. Nick Neave et al., "The Role of Attachment Style and Anthropomorphism in Predicting Hoarding Behaviours in a Non-Clinical Sample," *Personality and Individual Differences* 99 (2016): 35.

7. Lenny Van Rosmalen, René Van der Veer, and Frank Van der Horst, "Ainsworth's Strange Situation Procedure: The Origin of an Instrument," *Journal of the History of the Behavioral Sciences* 51, no. 3 (2015): 261–84, https://doi.org/10.1002/jhbs.21729.

8. Spangler and Grossman, "Biobehavioral Organization," 1446.

9. Tim Clinton and Gary Sibcy, *Attachments: Why You Love, Feel, and Act the Way You Do* (Nashville: Integrity, 2002), chap. 4.

10. Kuhnley, *The Mister Rogers Effect*, 64.

11. Gary Chapman, *The 5 Love Languages: The Secret to Love That Lasts* (Chicago: Northfield Publishing, 1992), loc. 65 of 208, Kindle.

12. Heike Winterheld, "Hiding Feelings for Whose Sake? Attachment Avoidance, Relationship Connectedness, and Protective Buffering Intentions," *Emotion* 17, no. 6 (2017): 965, https://doi.org/10.1037/emo0000291.

13. Len Fisher, "How Much Salt Is in a Human Body?," BBC Science Focus, accessed March 20, 2023, https://www.sciencefocus.com/the-human-body/how-much-salt-is-in-a-human-body/.

14. Knight et al., "Impact of Brief God Attachment."

15. "The One Question That Will Change Your Life," Amen Clinics, July 16, 2020, https://www.amenclinics.com/blog/the-one-question-that-will-change-your-life/.

16. Kuhnley, *The Mister Rogers Effect*, page 83 of 209, Kindle.

Chapter 7 The Networker

1. The Dancing Duo homepage, https://dancingduo.net/.

2. "Uptown Funk," featuring Bruno Mars, track 4 on Mark Ronson, *Uptown Special*, RCA, 2015.

3. John Gottman and Julie Gottman, *The Art and Science of Love* (workshop, March 10–11, 2022), https://www.gottman.com/couples/workshops/art-science-of-love/.

4. Gottman and Silver, *Seven Principles*, 10–11.

5. Kuhnley, *The Mister Rogers Effect*, 169.

6. Shaver, Belsky, and Brennan, "Adult Attachment Interview," 32.

7. Shaver, Belsky, and Brennan, "Adult Attachment Interview," 32.

8. Chapman, *5 Love Languages*, 151.

9. Paul S. Ciechanowski et al., "Attachment Theory: A Model for Health Care Utilization and Somatization," *Psychosomatic Medicine* 64, no. 4 (2002): 660; Donald G. Dutton and Katherine R. White, "Attachment Insecurity and Intimate Partner Violence," *Aggression and Violent Behavior* 17, no. 5 (2012): 475–81; Natacha Godbout et al., "Early Exposure to Violence, Relationship Violence, and Relationship Satisfaction in Adolescents and Emerging Adults: The Role of Romantic Attachment," *Psychological Trauma: Theory, Research, Practice, and Policy* 9, no. 2 (2017): 127, https://doi.org/10.1037/tra0000136.

10. Lachlan A. McWilliams and S. Jeffrey Bailey, "Associations between Adult Attachment Ratings and Health Conditions: Evidence from the National Comorbidity Survey Replication," *Health Psychology* 29, no. 4 (2010): 446, https://doi.org/10.1037/a0020061.

11. Erin M. Miga et al., "The Relation of Insecure Attachment States of Mind and Romantic Attachment Styles to Adolescent Aggression in Romantic Relationships," *Attachment & Human Development* 12, no. 5 (2010): 463–81, https://doi.org/10.1080/14616734.2010.501971.

12. Miga et al., "Relation of Insecure Attachment," 465.

13. McWilliams and Bailey, "Adult Attachment Ratings and Health Conditions," 452.

14. Ciechanowski et al., "Attachment Theory," 660.

15. E. Gail Horton et al., "Adult Attachment Style, Spirituality, and Religiosity among Individuals in Treatment for Substance Use Disorders," *Florida Public Health Review* 9, no. 16 (2012): 121, https://digitalcommons.unf.edu/cgi/viewcontent.cgi?article=1146&context=fphr.

16. Angela Rowe and Katherine B. Carnelley, "Attachment Style Differences in the Processing of Attachment-Relevant Information: Primed-Style Effects on Recall, Interpersonal Expectations, and Affect," *Personal Relationships* 10, no. 1 (2003): 59–60, https://doi.org/10.1111/1475-6811.00036.

17. Foster, Kernis, and Goldman, "Linking Adult Attachment to Self-Esteem Stability," 69–70; Stephanie A. Gamble and John E. Roberts, "Adolescents' Perceptions of Primary Caregivers and Cognitive Style: The Roles of Attachment Security and Gender," *Cognitive Therapy and Research* 29 (2005): 123, https://psycnet.apa.org/doi/10.1007/s10608-005-3160-7; Eunhyang Kim and Eunyoung Koh, "Avoidant Attachment and Smartphone Addiction in College Students: The Mediating Effects of Anxiety and Self-Esteem," *Computers in Human Behavior* 84 (2018): 264, https://doi.org/10.1016/j.chb.2018.02.037.

18. Abigail Millings et al., "School Connectedness, Peer Attachment, and Self-Esteem as Predictors of Adolescent Depression," *Journal of Adolescence* 35, no. 4 (2012): 1061, https://doi.org/10.1016/j.adolescence.2012.02.015.

19. Eilish Burke, Adam Danquah, and Katherine Berry, "A Qualitative Exploration of the Use of Attachment Theory in Adult Psychological Therapy," *Clinical Psychology & Psychotherapy* 23, no. 2 (2016): 142, https://doi.org/10.1002/cpp.1943; Susan M. Johnson, "A New Era for Couple Therapy: Theory, Research, and Practice in Concert," *Journal of Systemic Therapies* 26, no. 4 (2007): 5, https://doi.org/10.1521/jsyt.2007.26.4.5.

20. John Harrichand et al., "The Impact of Emotional Intelligence on Counselor Burnout," *Virginia Counselors Journal* 35 (Spring 2017): 44.

21. Lutz Jäncke, Franz Liem, and Susan Merillat, "Are Language Skills Related to Structural Features in Broca's and Wernicke's Area?," *European Journal of Neuroscience* 53, no. 4 (2021): 1132.

22. Daniel J. Siegel, "Toward an Interpersonal Neurobiology," 67.

23. Daniel Amen, *Change Your Brain, Change Your Life,* rev. ed. (New York: Harmony Books, 2015), 33.

24. Kuhnley and Sibcy, *Redeeming Attachment,* 55.

25. Bob Marvin, "Dr. Bob Marvin on Attachment & Developmental Pathway to Healing," YouTube video, posted by The Ainsworth Attachment Clinic & Circle of Security, November 18, 2013, https://www.youtube.com/watch?v=joDgWQwOWnI.

Chapter 8 The Path to Connection

1. Glenn I. Roisman et al., "Earned-Secure Attachment Status in Retrospect and Prospect," *Child Development* 73, no. 4 (2002): 1204–19, https://doi.org/10.1111/1467-8624.00467.

2. Roisman et al., "Earned-Secure Attachment," 1215.

3. Tim Clinton and Gary Sibcy with Sharon Hart Morris, "Love, Sex, and Marriage: Working Out Our Most Intimate Relationship," in *Attachments: Why You Love, Feel, and Act the Way You Do* (Brentwood, TN: Integrity Publishers, 2009), chap. 10.

4. Anita K. Kuhnley et al., "Creatively Increasing Empathy: The Impacts of an Online Empathy Workshop," *Journal of Creativity in Mental Health* 18, no. 1 (2023): 60–72, https://doi.org/10.1080/15401383.2021.1936328.

5. Hannah Hurnard, *Hinds' Feet on High Places* (Carol Stream, IL: Tyndale Momentum, 1979).

6. Steffany Gretzinger, "Out of Hiding (Father's Song)," *The Undoing,* track 3, produced by Bethel Music, 2014.

DR. ANITA KNIGHT KUHNLEY

Anita Knight Kuhnley, PhD, trains counselors and psychologists at Liberty University and serves as an adjunct professor of counseling in the School of Psychology and Counseling at her alma mater, Regent University, in Virginia Beach, VA. She teaches in the CACREP-accredited counseling program. Kuhnley enjoys journeying with students in the exploration of counseling research and the process of becoming. She has always loved Mister Rogers and aims to bring the Mister Rogers Effect to each of her classes. Kuhnley earned her doctorate in counselor education and supervision and her MA in community counseling from Regent. She is also certified as a highly reliable coder of the Adult Attachment Interview (AAI) through Mary Main and Eric Hesse's UC Berkeley AAI coder certification program. With her husband and their two poodle pups, she lives in Northeast Florida and loves to adventure anywhere she can see the deep blue sea. Kuhnley is also the author of several books, including *Redeeming Attachment, Counseling Women, Research-Based Counseling Skills,* and *The Mister Rogers Effect.* For more information, visit her website, DrAnitaKuhnley.com.